Andrew Hale Feinstein   John M. Stefanelli   Gael D. Hancock

Study Guide to Accompany

Purchasing

Selection and Procurement for the Hospitality Industry

Seventh Edition

JOHN WILEY & SONS, INC.

Published by John Wiley and Sons, Inc., Hoboken, New Jersey.
Published simultaneously in Canada.

Wiley Bicentennial Logo Design by Richard J. Pacifico.

For general information on our other products and services, or technical support, please contact our Customer Care Department within the United States at 800-762-2974, outside the United States at 317-572-3993 or fax 317-572-4002.

Wiley also publishes its books in a variety of electronic formats. Some content that appears in print may not be available in electronic books.

For more information about Wiley products, visit our Web site at http://*www.wiley.com*.

Library of Congress Cataloging-in-Publication Data:

ISBN 13: 978-0-470-14054-3

Printed in the United States of America

10   9   8   7   6   5   4   3   2

Table of Contents

Introduction

Purchasing is one of the most important activities in the hospitality industry, for without it there would no sheets for the beds, no talent in the theaters, no liquor at the bar and no keys to the rooms. Not everyone is going to leave this class wanting to be a buyer for a large corporation, but if you stay in the hospitality field, you will almost inevitably find yourself working with a purchasing agent in some capacity. You may need him or her to order an item for you. You may be hiring a purchasing agent. You may be providing accounting information to a buyer. You may be selling products or services to a buyer. The list is endless.

The new edition of this textbook was developed to help you learn the basics of purchasing. A glossary was created to help you understand this industry-specific terminology. Sidebar articles were added to give you a more personal look at this interesting profession. Color was added to highlight information and add interest.

In this study guide, you will find a detailed outline of each chapter and questions to help you review the materials. Question types include true/false, fill-in-the-blank and multiple choice. There are also two or three thought questions under the heading, "Apply Your Knowledge." An answer key has been provided at the end of the book for all questions except the "Apply Your Knowledge" section.

Before you begin a chapter, go to the back of the chapter and make a mental note of the "Key Words and Concepts." This will help you recognize the important terms as you study. When you read a question, try not to hurriedly answer the question and move on to the next. For example, in Chapter 8, one of the questions is as follows:

> Which of the following items would not normally be found on a product specification?
> a. country of origin
> b. package size
> c. allowable number of returns and stockouts
> d. U.S. quality grade

The answer is "c," but rather than just moving to the next question, you might think to yourself, "The answer is 'c' because 'allowable number of returns and stockouts' would appear on a purchase specification rather than a product specification." Thinking through the question in this manner will help you confirm the definition in your head of not one, but two of the important terms in the book.

Enjoy your studies!

Chapter 1 The Concepts of Selection and Procurement

After reading this chapter, you should be able to:

- Describe the difference between "purchasing," "selection," and "procurement."
- Identify commercial and non-commercial hospitality operations.
- Explain how technology and e-commerce applications are changing the purchasing industry.
- Explain how purchasing functions differ in hospitality operations of varying sizes.

Outline

1. Introduction
   - All jobs in the hospitality industry involve purchasing in one way or another
   - The conventional definition of "purchasing" which means simply paying for an item or service, is too restrictive
   - Two terms that define a buyer's activities are more applicable:
     - Selection: choosing an item or service from a number of different alternatives on a number of different levels
     - Procurement: the process of obtaining the goods or services including
       - determination of need
       - administering purchase contracts
       - completing the purchase
       - receiving and storing shipments
   - Procurement makes up the bulk of a buyer's job
     - How much to buy
     - Best price
     - Best time
     - Product/service meets needs of the organization
   - Internet aids procurement process
     - Easy to complete electric commerce transactions (e-commerce)
     - B2B e-commerce refers to business-to-business transactions
     - B2C e-commerce refers to business to consumer transactions
     - E-procurement is the term for transactions that focus specifically on procurement activities
     - Instill (www.instill.com) is a company that specializes in developing e-procurement applications for the foodservice industry
     - Avendra (www.avendra.com) is a company that does the same for the hotel industry
   - Three types of hospitality operations
     - Commercial–profit oriented
     - Institutional–facilities that operate on a break-even basis (non-commercial)
     - Military–operations that include troop feeding and housing (non-commercial)
2. Purchasing Functions in Different Types of Hospitality Operations
   - Small independent operations
     - Run by an owner-manager who does buying
     - Owner-manager oversees receiving, paying the bills
   - Medium independent operations
     - Usually involves more than one person in the purchasing process
     - General manager usually coordinates purchasing activities of department heads (dining room manager, bartender, etc.)
   - Large independent operations
     - May employ a full-time buyer
     - May use a designated employee as buyer from each department
   - Competing with larger markets

- o E-procurement technology has leveled the playing field in terms of competitive pricing
  - ▪ Foodservice central (www.foodservicecentral.com)
  - ▪ Network for B2B Professionals (www.b2business.net)
  - ▪ Amphire (www.amphire.com)
- o Cooperative buying
- o Aggregate purchasing companies
  - ▪ Do not buy or sell products
  - ▪ Negotiate contracts on behalf of members: restaurants, hotels, management companies, resorts and Real Estate Investment Trusts (REITs)
  - ▪ Participants receive listing of emails and phone numbers of suppliers with brief description of programs negotiated on purchasing companies' behalf
- • Multi-units and franchises
  - o Centrally located vice president of purchasing
  - o May have one or more central distribution points (possibly a commissary)
  - o Managers may purchase minimal amount from national or local suppliers as approved by vice president

True/False

T F 1. "Purchasing" is an accurate term for the range of activities required of a purchasing manager.

T F 2. Most operations, regardless of the size, have full-time buyers.

T F 3. Small hospitality operations are now better able to compete with larger operations thanks to group purchasing organizations and other group-buying opportunities.

T F 4. Franchise operators may be more restricted in their buying options due to company policies and procedures.

T F 5. Buyers almost never have to work with people outside their department.

T F 6. Group purchasing organizations, or GPOs, keep large inventories of products for sale.

T F 7. Today buyers for even small operations have access to goods from all over the world.

T F 8. A foodservice operation in a correctional facility is considered to be a noncommercial operation.

T F 9. A buyer is responsible for ensuring that the purchased good or service meets the needs of the organization.

T F 10. In a large independent operation, each department may have its own buyer.

Fill-in-the-Blank

1. In the hospitality industry, _____ and _____ are the two key activities of a buyer. _____ is the choosing of the item among a number of alternatives including for example, grade, amount of processing (fresh or frozen) or supplier. _____ is the exchange of money for the item and all of the steps that involves including the purchasing contract, receipt of goods on property, storage, and others.

2. List the three types of hospitality operations below, indicate whether they are commercial or non-commercial and give an example of each:

Hospitality Operation	Commercial/Non-Commercial	Example
_____	_____	_____
_____	_____	_____
_____	_____	_____

3. Most procurement functions can now be accomplished with a few clicks of a mouse thanks to the Internet. There are two kinds of electronic or e-commerce, _____ with the acronym of _____ and _____ with the acronym of _____. Amazon.com is a good example of _____ e-commerce. E-commerce focusing on procurement is known as _____.

4. The electronic or e-marketplace has made it possible for small operations to easily take advantage of bulk-purchase prices. _____ is one way to accomplish this where members might rotate the buying responsibilities among themselves. Another example of this type of organization is known as a referral group where independents join together to send business to one another.

5. A company that gathers together procurement processes is called a _____ or _____. These organizations do not sell products themselves, instead they negotiate contracts on behalf of hotels, restaurants, Real Estate Investment Trusts (REITs), etc. Members in turn will access the approved suppliers or distributors through a private portal to make their purchases.

6. A _____ and a _____ are both terms for a distribution area that might be utilized by a franchise or multi-unit operation.

Multiple Choice
1. Which of the following would fall into the commercial category of hospitality operations?
   a. school cafeteria
   b. food service at an assisted living facility
   c. military operation
   d. none of the above

2. Which of the following activities falls under the heading of selection?
   a. determining how much to pay for a product/service
   b. deciding when to place an order
   c. deciding whether to order organic produce
   d. choosing a supplier

3. E-procurement can be used by:
   a. small companies
   b. medium companies
   c. only independent companies
   d. all companies

4. What type of buyer system might one expect to find in a small independent operation?
   a. a buyer or steward for each department
   b. numerous buyers at a centralized location
   c. owner-manger doing the purchasing
   d. none of the above

5. What type of buyer system might one expect to find in a large independent operation?
   a. a buyer or steward for each department
   b. numerous buyers at a centralized location
   c. a owner-manager doing the buying
   d. none of the above

Apply Your Knowledge

1. Examine the selection and procurement activities of an owner-manager and the local manager of a multi-unit operation. Describe how they are different and how they are alike.

2. Discuss how a co-op buying operation is different from a group purchasing organization or aggregate buying company.

3. Describe how e-commerce creates a "level playing field" for all sizes of hospitality operations.

Chapter 2
Technology Applications in Purchasing
After reading this chapter, you should be able to:
- Explain how hospitality operators use technologies in the selection, procurement, and inventory process.

Outline
1. Technologies that Distributors Use
   - Distributors are the "middlemen" between the retailer and the source
   - Need to keep track of customers, sources, costs and specifications
   - Customer databases
     o Use specialized software
     o Help predict customers' product needs
     o Provide marketing information
     o Help forecast the number of hospitality operations that might open in a particular area
     o Database management often handled under Customer Relations Management (CRM) strategy
   - Ordering systems
     o Software applications to facilitate the sales process
     o With some systems, customers can access prices, product availability
     o Also called "web order entry systems"
     o Distributors usually provide these services free of charge
     o U.S. Foodservice (www.usfood.com) and Sysco (www.esysco.net) are two of the largest broadline foodservice distributors in the United States
   - Global positioning systems (GPS)
     o Used by distributors with logistics and mapping software to develop routes for delivery vehicles; known as GPS vehicle tracking system
     o Fleet management software can be used to determine most efficient route to take and optimum number of vehicles
       ▪ Estimates driver downtime
       ▪ Estimates amount of product that should be delivered per hour
       ▪ Estimates expected loading and unloading times
     o Other software can track delivery errors, discrepancies and customer complaints or comments
     o Enables distributor to minimize delivery costs
   - RFIDs – radio frequency identification tags
     o Predicted to dramatically change management and distribution of products
     o Definition: tiny microchips that can be used for tracking
       ▪ Example: RFIDS attached to apples can monitor location and temperature throughout the delivery process
2. Technologies that Buyers Use
   - Fax machines
     o Revolutionized procurement process in 1980s
     o Reduced confusion and mistakes of verbal orders
     o Printed output could be stored especially after advent of plain paper fax machines in 1990s
   - Personal computers
     o Most powerful tool for buyer
     o Spreadsheet software programs allowed for management of massive amounts of data
     o When connected to the Internet, allow for instant access to accurate cost information

- Computerized point-of-sale systems (POS systems)
  - Tabulate and store sales data
  - Allow management to see real-time sales data
  - Often interface with inventory systems that automatically delete from inventory the standard amount of ingredients used to make menu items
  - Provides management with theoretical inventory usage figure to compare with actual inventory counts
  - Some systems can actually send purchase orders to a distributor based on sales
- Bar code reader
  - Bar code labels are a series of vertical lines of varying thicknesses separated by blank spaces
  - Lines and spaces called "elements" give a bar code reader an identification code or ID
  - Bar code elements, IDs and product information are based on a standard that associate these pieces of information
  - The Universal Product Code (UPC) is the most commonly used standard
  - When products in inventory have a bar code, a reader can be used to download inventory counts to a computer; many bar code readers are now wireless
  - Can be used to accurately assess liquor inventory; NUVO Technologies (www.barvision.com) has developed free-pour spouts with radio transmitters that send pouring information directly to POS systems
- Product identification and specifications
  - CD versions of specifications manuals with search capabilities
  - CDs that allow buyers to search database indexes with thousands of product categories to locate information about distributors
    - Example: The Food and Beverage Market Place, formerly the Thomas Food Industry Register (TFIR), has database of more than 40,000 company listings and nearly 6,000 product categories
- Product ordering
  - Direct ordering using an e-marketplace
    - Reduces time and labor on buyers' and distributors' ends
    - Distributor benefits from the development of a loyal customer, also known as a house account or prime-vendor account, who likes the easy-order system
  - E-marketplaces allow for negotiation of contractual pricing agreements prior to ordering
    - Buyer submits request for quote (RFQ) to chosen vendors
    - Vendors respond with a price
    - Buyer chooses vendor based on price, delivery times, availability or other criterion
  - After prices have been established, purchasing managers can allow departmental managers to order items directly through the e-marketplace
  - An e-marketplace allows for custom formatting of information, for example one could view hot dogs by size, ingredients and brands
- Inventory-tracking and storage management
  - Many managers use self-developed spreadsheets for inventory control
  - Another option: Materials and Management System (www.agilysys.com) by Agilysys
  - Many inventory management systems can be linked to the POS system
  - Specialists can develop customized applications to meet the needs of any operation
- Internet
  - Streamlines operations
  - Allows for instant communications

- o Developed in the late 1960s at the Advanced Research Projects Agency network of the U.S. Department of Defense
- Electronic mail (e-mail)
  - o Allows for attached files
  - o Creates an easy-to-search record
- Newsgroups and mailing lists
  - o Connect people of similar interests
  - o Allow for quick answers to specific questions
- World wide web
  - o Graphical interface that allows for information to be accessed via hyperlinks
  - o Sites for hospitality buyer: daily news about the hospitality industry
  - o Decision-making information on fresh produce and area weather reports
  - o Information to help buyers spec out products (example: California Avocado Commission, www.avocado.org)
  - o Recipes are available
- Instant and text messaging
  - o Allows for instant communication using computers, cell phones or personal digital assistants (PDAs)
  - o Files can be attached

3. What Lies Ahead
- Technology will help operators overcome challenges of competitive markets, slimmer profit margins and a shrinking labor force
- Distributors may bear burden of providing hospitality operators with technology for procurement
- Distributors may be more actively involved with customers, helping develop and evaluate menus, substitution possibilities, inventory management procedures, marketing strategies
- Hospitality operators may do more one-stop shopping

4. Roadblocks to adoption of e-procurement
- Companies developing B2B software are now trading at a fraction of their former heyday prices, or gone entirely due in part to unanticipated slowness of hospitality industry to adopt e-procurement
- Understanding the hospitality industry
  - o Most U.S. restaurants are independent operations
  - o Owner/operators have limited time to spend selecting/procuring products
  - o Lack of attention in this area can result in failure (26 percent of restaurants fail in the first year of operation)
  - o Industry is still reliant on the fax machine rather than using e-procurement
  - o In 2001 only 60 percent of the table-service operations and 25 percent of quick-service operations had access to the Internet
  - o Due to time constraints, many independent operators use one-stop shopping and accept whatever prices are given them
  - o In contrast, multi-unit and large independents provide technological resources to the supply manager to assist in product selection and procurement
  - o The challenges for these organizations are not time constraints, but the management of people and information
    - Determining departmental product needs
    - Assisting in the development of specifications
    - Identifying acceptable products
    - Approving requisitions
    - Managing buyers
    - Vast amounts of paperwork

- Entities that affect the hospitality e-procurement process
    - Employees
        - Resistance due to situational variables
            - Fear of losing position of power or the position itself
            - Reluctance to change habits
            - Issues surrounding inertia
            - Disruption in the organizational culture and climate
            - Experience with prior failed change efforts
            - Peer group pressure
            - Lack of participation in the process
        - Social-psychological and personality variables
            - Cognitive dissonance
            - Risk aversion
            - Lack of faith or confidence
            - Conservative outlook
            - "What's in it for me" outlook
        - Fear of or resistance to technological advancement
    - Suppliers
        - Can hinder flow of e-procurement due to fear of disintermediation; a not unwarranted fear
        - Unwillingness to let go of expensive, proprietary computer systems
        - Reluctant to make additional investments
    - Organizations
        - Issue of standardization of product identification
            - Efficient Foodservice Response (EFT) initiative aimed at eliminating problem
                - Hindered by inability to develop common terminology for products
                - Another problem—few companies use bar codes on produce
        - Organizations concerned about doing business with third-party dot-com companies
        - Many organizations are small and lack time, personnel and equipment to use e-procurement solutions
        - Organizations must deal with depersonalization—managers believe that online purchasing will depersonalize the process
5. The Future of E-procurement
    - Moving toward a free market where even the smallest operators can realize benefits in product selection, price and use of their time
        - Overcoming roadblocks
            - Employees
                - Communication is key
                - Involvement in the process
            - Suppliers
                - Many buyers will not do business with suppliers who do not have e-commerce connections
                - Services and technologies provided will differentiate suppliers more than product

- Organizations
  - Hospitality operators will see benefits of e-procurement as they experience slimmer profit margins, a shrinking labor force and time constraints
  - Further development of identification standards

True/False

T F 1.   Employees are always eager to embrace new technologies and new ideas.

T F 2.   Fleet management software can be used to determine the most efficient delivery routes and the optimal number of vehicles.

T F 3.   The simple fax machine revolutionized the order-taking and receiving process in the 1980s.

T F 4.   Food-marketing boards such as the California Avocado Commission (www.avocado.org) are excellent sources of product information.

T F 5.   A buyer may want to join a newsgroup (also known as an interest group) so he/she can quickly obtain specific information.

T F 6.   The Universal Product Code (UPC) is not used very much by the hospitality industry.

T F 7.   Many inventory management software packages can cost recipes, analyze a recipe's nutritional content, calculate food and beverage costs, and evaluate a food item's sales history.

T F 8.   Suppliers worry about disintermediation or loss of sales when buyers become more able to connect directly with product sources due to e-procurement.

T F 9.   "Future Shock" was a concept of Alvin Toffler that predicted that people will fear technological advancements and won't be able to adjust physically, mentally or socially ensuing changes.

T F 10.   The buyer often purchases software applications to facilitate the sales process and provides them to his/her suppliers.

Fill-in-the-Blank

1.   A distributor is the _____ or _____ between a source and retailer. Distributors must keep up with huge amounts of data in relation to products and clients. Customer data is often tracked using a _____ or _____ (acronym) strategy.

2.   The location of an Internet site is known as a _____ or _____ (acronym).

3.   The most active part of the Internet is known as the _____. A website that provides detailed information on fresh produce farming, distribution and related weather conditions was developed by the _____. This information can help a buyer decide whether to leave an item, such as asparagus, on the menu because of an extended growing season.

4.   In any industry, it is important to capture sales data. _____ systems can capture and analyze great amounts of data very quickly. Most of these systems now have touch-screen technology and some are now even wireless and can be carried to the table by waitstaff where orders are immediately sent to the screen in the bar or kitchen.

5.   In the buyer/supplier relationship, a house account is to a vendor as a _____ is to a buyer.

6.   Any time that the intermediary or "middleman" is cut out of the process it is known as _____. This can happen when a buyer goes directly to the source for a product.

7.   _____ or _____ (acronym), are tiny microchips that can be attached to products for tracking purposes. Some can monitor temperature throughout the shipping process.

8.   _____ information helps buyers "spec out" or compare similar products. Much of this information is now available online and in CD versions.

9.   In 1994, the _____ or _____ (acronym) was started to begin the process of developing identification standards for foodservice products.

10. _____ are organizations, usually centered around a specific product, that provide information about that product to buyers and consumers. The Australian Pork Corporation is an example of such an organization.

Multiple Choice
1.   This piece of equipment, that came on the scene in the 1980s, dramatically changed purchasing in the hospitality industry.
     a. fax machine
     b. bar code reader
     c. plain paper printer
     d. word processing systems

2.   Which of the following is one of the reasons e-procurement has not been universally embraced by the hospitality industry:
     a. fear of losing position of power (employee)
     b. confidence about keeping clients (supplier)
     c. eagerness to make the investment (supplier)
     d. failure to understand its advantages (organization)

3. Which of the following is not a step in the inventory management process?
     a. list new products to be researched
     b. list all products in inventory (using a spreadsheet)
     c. physically count storeroom and in-process inventories
     d. calculate cost of goods sold

4.   Of the following, which is not an advantage of purchasing through an e-marketplace?
     a. ability to search great amounts of data for a specific product
     b. ability to connect with multiple suppliers
     c. ability to negotiate prices before the order is placed
     d. ability to remain anonymous throughout the purchasing process

5. A buyer wanting to streamline his inventory process might invest in:
    a. RFIDs
    b. bar code scanners
    c. The Materials and Management System by Agilysis
    d. all of the above

6. One of a buyer's tasks is to spec out products. A buyer might use all but which of the following to gain product information:
    a. USDA's website
    b. marketing boards
    c. point-of-sale systems
    d. newsgroups

7. Which of the following would you not expect to find on an end-of-month profit and loss report?
    a. beginning inventory
    b. employee requests for new products
    c. purchases
    d. ending inventory

8. A savvy supplier might provide daily product information in a variety of ways. Which of the following would a technology-phobic buyer probably choose?
    a. quotes directly entered into buyer-supplied templates
    b. quotes distributed through an e-procurement application
    c. quotes delivered the preceding day by the supplier's delivery person
    d. quotes delivered via fax machine

9. An online ordering system developed by a supplier and provided to a buyer is called:
    a. a web order entry system
    b. an inventory control system
    c. an order-placing template
    d. none of the above

10. Of the following scenarios, which is least likely to happen?
    a. suppliers will continue to research and provide Internet-based ordering systems
    b. buyers will work together to create their own ordering systems
    c. software systems will be developed that further refine the inventory management process
    d. buyers will choose suppliers as much on the basis of product offerings as on the technology they provide to enhance ordering and product research

Apply Your Knowledge
1. Consider the concern that technology will "depersonalize" the channel of distribution. Discuss these issues and offer some solutions to this perceived problem.

2. Imagine that you are an owner/manager and have purchased a new inventory management system that interfaces with a new point-of-sale system. Discuss how you would introduce these systems to your employees and how you would help them overcome their hesitancy to embrace such changes.
3. Taking into consideration your own knowledge of today's technology—the Internet, world wide web, etc.—do you see additional ways that the ordering, inventory and sales operations can be streamlined. Explain.

Chapter 3
Distribution Systems
After studying this chapter, you should be able to:
- Outline the distribution systems in the hospitality industry.
- Explain the economic values added to products and services as they journey through the channel of distribution.
- Evaluate the determination of optimal values and supplier services in the hospitality industry.

Outline
1. Distribution System for Food, Non-Alcoholic Beverages, and Nonfood Supplies
   - Thousands of primary sources and intermediaries compete to serve approximately 925,000 foodservice and 47,598 lodging operations in the United States
   - Primary sources
     o Growers
     o Manufacturers
       ▪ Food products
       ▪ Nonfood products
     o Processors or fabricators
       ▪ Food products only
   - Intermediaries
     o Distributors: merchant wholesalers; buy directly from primary sources; earn profit on resale
       ▪ Specialty distributor: carries only one type or class of item (i.e., coffee)
       ▪ Full-line distributor: carries food and nonfood items
       ▪ Broadline distributor: carries food, nonfood items and equipment
     o Broker: works for primary sources; job is to promote products; doesn't carry inventory; earns commission
     o Manufacturer's representative: function similar to broker but may carry product; "reps" as they're called, are most often found in the equipment and furnishings trade and brokers are found in the food and nonfood trade
     o Manufacturer's agent: similar to manufacturer's representatives, but employed directly by primary sources; often a manufacturer's agent is another primary source that has agreed to take on the marketing efforts of a source too small to market on its own
     o Commissary: usually owned by large foodservice operation; processes food products to exact specifications and sells and ships to company-owned restaurants or franchisees
     o Wholesale clubs—"cash and carry" operations patronized by small businesses that do not buy enough to warrant deliveries from distributors
     o Buying clubs—groups of purchasers who work together to take advantage of competitive prices by placing orders larger than they could do independently
     o E-commerce enabler: provides software that allows primary sources, intermediaries and buyers to communicate and develop procurement relationships
2. Distribution System for Beer, Wine and Distilled Spirits
   - Sources
     o Brewers
     o Winemakers
     o Distillers
   - Intermediaries
     o Importers-wholesalers: import alcoholic products into the United States and into individual states; most act as liquor distributors, buying from a number of primary sources and then reselling to retail operations

- o Distributor: specialized wholesalers who operate under specific laws; most are prohibited by "tied-house" from becoming either primary source or retailer
- o Alcohol beverage commission: liquor control authority in a state
  - ▪ Control state: liquor is sold by the state itself
  - ▪ License state: liquor sales are licensed to importers-wholesalers, distributors and retailers
3. Distribution System for Furniture, Fixtures and Equipment (FFE)
   - Source: manufacturers
   - Intermediaries
     - o Dealers: usually function like a food distributor
       - ▪ Catalog house: keeps very little inventory and sells from catalogs (often online); handles the order, delivery, setup
       - ▪ Storefront dealer: also called "discount operation"; carries a small inventory, usually of small portable items
       - ▪ Heavy equipment dealer
       - ▪ Full-service dealer: carries full range of FFE and provides all end-user services
     - o Brokers: similar to food brokers
     - o Designers: contract with the hospitality operation and serve as consultants; order FFE and ensure timely installation
     - o Architects: similar to designers
     - o Construction contractors: similar to designers
     - o Distributors: food and nonfood distributors often carry common FFE items
     - o Leasing Companies
4. Distribution Systems for Services
   - Services such as advertising, consulting and waste removal, are often provided by local operations
5. What Happens Throughout the Channel of Distribution
   - Time value
     - o Storage of product
     - o Credit
     - o Wine prices – the price goes up as the wine ages
   - Form value
     - o Most expensive value added to a product
     - o Turning a raw ingredient into something different, i.e., flour into bread
     - o Cost includes packaging
   - Place value
     - o Cost of delivery
     - o Frozen or refrigerated foods increase this cost
   - Information value
     - o Directions for use
     - o Training
   - Supplier services value
     - o A supplier who will rush over an item in his/her car in an emergency
     - o An accountant who quickly prepares an important report
6. Ultimate value: the sum of a product's quality and the values added to it
7. The Buyer's Place in the Channel of Distribution
   - Eliminating the intermediary
     - o Some buyers for large operations go around the distributor and buy directly from the primary source

- Some take deliveries at central-distribution centers, perhaps add value to the product in commissaries (clean, cut and package raw vegetables) and deliver to their restaurants or hotel properties in their own vehicles
- Companies claim cost savings, more control over product, improved coordination and ability to overcome suppliers' lack of technological capabilities as advantages
- In support of the intermediary
  - Other buyers enjoy the services provided by distributors (new product information, purchase discounts, etc.)
  - Few have been able to increase profits by eliminating the middleman
  - Danger of losing sight of the operation's major business
8. The Optimal Economic Values and Supplier Services
  - In recessionary times, buyers start looking for ways to cut costs
  - As-purchased (AP) price of a pre-portioned steak vs. the AP price of a side of beef
9. Selecting Economic Values
  - Buyers have input into which economic values their company will provide for itself, but managers have the final say
  - Does the manager really want to get into the meat packing business? Or buy a truck?
  - Will antitrust problems arise?
  - What will company employees say about taking on additional burdens?
10. Selecting Supplier Services
  - Buyers have some say in selecting supplier services and thus can affect the AP price
  - Must balance cost savings against hidden costs

True/False

T F 1. Processors produce both food products and non-food items.

T F 2. A distributor purchases directly from growers, processors or manufacturers.

T F 3. An e-commerce enabler is one who provides software applications to facilitate online buying and selling of products.

T F 4. A retailer is one who sells a good or service directly to the consumer.

T F 5. A pre-cut steak is usually cheaper per pound than it would be if an entire side of beef were purchased and cut into steaks at the restaurant.

T F 6. Wholesale clubs are a primary purchasing source for large hotel chains.

T F 7. In a control state, buyers must follow the purchasing, bill-paying and receiving guidelines for liquor as set out by the state.

T F 8. A grower might sell to both a restaurant chain and to a processor.

T F 9. There are three major sources for alcohol products: brewers, wine makers and distillers.

T F 10. A broker does not usually carry products for re-sale.

Fill-in-the-Blank

1. _____ is a state's governing body that oversees the distribution and sale of alcohol products.

2. A _____ distributor is one who carries food, non-food items, equipment and possibly even furniture.

3. A _____ is a small furniture dealer that carries a minimal amount of inventory and usually specializes in small types of furniture, fixtures and equipment (FFE).

4. In the early 1990s, the foodservice industry initiated a global effort to explore methods for cost reduction. The result was the _____ initiative. Two similar initiatives in the warehouse industry were the _____ and the _____ methods.

5. In many states, liquor distributors will operate in _____ where they are the only suppliers to carry specific brands. This results in little competition among wholesale liquor distributors.

6. In most states, _____ prohibit wholesale liquor distributors from becoming retailers.

7. A _____ distributor is one who sells food and non-food items. A _____ dealer is one who typically carries a full FFE line.

8. A _____ is a place where foods are processed to the exact specifications of a company. From there, foods are sold and shipped to company-owned restaurants or franchises.

9. A broker provides the sales effort and the distributor provides the _____ or everything but the sales effort.

10. _____ is the term for purchasing an item from a primary source such as fresh spinach directly from the grower.

Multiple Choice

1. Which of the items below is not considered to be an economic value?
   a. time value
   b. form value
   c. re-sale value
   d. information value

2. Foods that have been processed, such as pizza are often called efficiency foods. These foods may also be called
   a. convenience or value added foods
   b. convenience or premium
   c. convertible or value added foods
   d. convertible or premium foods

3. Which of the following would not be considered to be an intermediary or middleman?
   a. distributor
   b. grower
   c. broker
   d. importer

4.   Which of the following is a supplier service?
        a. delivery of goods
        b. 30 to 45 days of credit
        c. storage of goods till they're needed
        d. all of the above

5.   "Cash and carry" is a concept most associated with
        a. catalog houses
        b. buying clubs
        c. wholesale clubs
        d. commissaries

6.   Which of the following does not fit the description of a broker:
        a. generates enthusiasm for a product
        b. earns a sales commission
        c. hands off the customer to the distributor for end-user services
        d. carries a number of products

7.   A distributor who carries only one type or classification of product would be a
        a. specialty distributor
        b. full-line distributor
        c. broadline distributor
        d. narrow-line distributor

8.   An order of fresh vegetables delivered to the loading dock of your restaurant specifically exhibits what kind of value?
        a. time value
        b. place value
        c. form value
        d. information value

9.   Which of the items below is probably not a reason a company would eliminate the distributor and purchase items directly from a primary source?
        a. improved coordination
        b. increased control over product
        c. cost savings
        d. eliminates paperwork

10. Why would a company be leery of taking responsibility for some of the economic values of a product?
        a. hesitation to take on additional projects or expenses (buy a truck for example)
        b. awareness of antitrust issues
        c. employee backlash
        d. all of the above

Apply Your Knowledge
1.   Trace the path a tomato would take through the channel of distribution as it becomes a catsup packet in a fast food restaurant. Discuss how the four economic values add to the cost of the packet and how that cost differs from the price of the original tomato.

16

2.	How important is the information value of a product? Imagine that you are a restaurant owner and have just purchased a new pour-through alcohol dispensing system and a new oven. Discuss the importance of "information value" in relation to both of these purchases.

3.	As a buyer in a medium-size hotel, you have been asked to look at ways to reduce the costs of cleaning supplies. One of your options is to purchases cleaning fluids in 50-gallon drums and then recant the liquids into usable spray bottles. Discuss the pros and cons of this option.

Chapter 4
Forces Affecting the Distribution Systems
After reading this chapter, you should be able to:
- Identify the economic forces that affect the channel of distribution.
- Identify the political forces that affect the channel of distribution.
- Identify the legal restrictions that affect the channel of distribution.
- Identify the technological advances that affect the channel of distribution.

Outline
1. Introduction
   - Several forces affect the price and availability of products
2. Economic Force
   - Supply-and-demand considerations affect purchase prices
   - If the amount available exceeds the demand, the price drops until the product is sold
   - As products move along the channel, they acquire different values
   - A seller begins to exercise control over the price and does not always need to accept the price determined by supply-and-demand
   - Sellers emphasize overall product value
   - The perceived EP cost is the final cost to the customer of providing a finished meal
      o It is not equal to the AP price
      o Traditionally, the EP cost of food includes only the food-ingredient cost
      o Here we refer to the EP cost as the as-served cost of food or beverages
   - Sellers' ability to manipulate the value equation and the supply-and-demand conditions is referred to as "monopolistic competition"
      o Most common type of marketing environment found throughout the hospitality industry
      o All members of the distribution system strive to highlight value over price
      o Buyers must pay a bit more for a unique set of quality, supplier services and EP cost
3. Political Force
   - Large suppliers and hospitality enterprises have influence in state legislatures and the U.S. Congress
   - Most simply join a local hospitality association and/or chamber of commerce
   - "Unwritten laws" can affect a channel member's behavior
   - The political force influences product availability, prices and channel member behavior
4. Ethical Force
   - Some unethical behaviors include:
      o Rebates
      o Kickbacks
   - Control systems can quickly detect the inflation of cost
   - Several professional purchasing associations have codes of ethics
      o All buyers and supervisors of buyers should be familiar with these codes
   - Legislators devote considerable attention to selling and buying practices
5. Legal Force
   - The Sherman Antitrust Act (1890)
      o The United State's first piece of antitrust legislation
      o Forbids any action that tends to eliminate or severely reduce competition
   - Meat safety legislation
      o In 1906, Upton Sinclair depicted unsanitary conditions in the meat packing industry in his book *The Jungle*
      o The book led to a severe decline in meat consumption

- Forced the federal government to pass the Pure Food Act (1906) and the Federal Meat Inspection Act (1906)
- These acts gave the U.S. Department of Agriculture inspection powers throughout the channels of distribution
- The meat-inspection legislation requires continuous ante mortem and postmortem inspection of all meat intended for interstate and international commerce
- The required inspection of poultry did not take effect until the passage of the Poultry Products Inspection Act (1957)
- Ralph Nader focused attention on abuses in the meat industry, resulting in passage of the Wholesome Meat Act (1967)
  - Current USDA food-safety authority rests on a series of legislation based primarily on the Wholesome Meat Act (1967), the Poultry Products Inspection Act (1957) and the Wholesome Poultry Products Act (1968)
- The USDA enforces chemical residue standards and the standards dealing with wholesomeness, general sanitation, packaging and labeling
- In 1996, the Wholesome Meat Act and the Wholesome Poultry Act added a Pathogen Reduction/Hazard Analysis Critical Control Points (HACCP) Rule
  - HACCP requires food processors to identify places within their production cycle where items can become contaminated and institute procedures to ensure food safety
- The Food Safety Inspection Service covers the voluntary inspection for animals not covered under mandatory inspection
- The Federal Food, Drug, and Cosmetic Act (1906)
  - Covers majority of food and drug regulation in the United States
  - Congress created the Food and Drug Administration (FDA) to administer this law
  - The FDA is responsible for random inspections of food processing plants in the United States
  - Cosmetics-Devices Act (1938)
    - Gave the FDA injunctive power and the authority to set food standards
    - FDA has the power to remove from the marketplace any product that does not meet agency standards
  - The FFDCA was amended by the Food Quality Protection Act in 1996
    - Provided a single safety standard for pesticide residuals in foods
- Seafood safety legislation
  - Seafood is not subject to mandatory, continuous inspection
  - In 1997, the FDA established HACCP requirements for all processors involved in interstate commerce and/or the importing of seafood
  - For a fee, a fish processor can obtain continuous inspection of its processing plant from the National Oceanic and Atmospheric Administration (NOAA)
  - Seafood is subject to the provisions of the FFDCA
    - This law permits the FDA to periodically inspect fish
  - The FDA has the authority to examine seafood in interstate commerce and, if the product is defective, to seize it and prohibit its sale
  - A cooperative program among state and federal agencies supervises beds of water used to grow and harvest shellfish
    - Interstate Shellfish Sanitation Conference
  - Some seafood products are subject to legislation that contributes to a safe, wholesome environment
    - 1992 Marine Mammal Protection Act
- Federal Trade Commission (1914), Amended by the Wheeler-Lea Act (1938)

- o The FTC deals with advertising, deceptive promotions, monopolies, and unprofessional misconduct in the marketplace
  - o Established primarily to clarify and enhance the Sherman Act
- The Clayton Act (1914)
  - o Another attempt by congress to increase the federal government's control over antitrust violations
  - o Two illegal activities are covered in this act
    - ▪ Tying agreements
    - ▪ Exclusive dealing
- Perishable Agricultural Commodities Act (1930)
  - o Controls interstate commerce by prohibiting unfair and fraudulent practices in the sale of fresh and frozen produce
- Agricultural Adjustment Act (1933) and Agricultural Marketing Agreement Act (1937)
  - o Permits primary sources and intermediaries to work to solve marketing problems and ensure a steady flow of perishable products
- The Robinson-Patman Act (1936)
  - o Known as the "small-business protection act"
  - o Designed to further enhance the power of the federal government to control antitrust violations
  - o Addressed three specific loopholes:
    - ▪ Promotional loopholes
    - ▪ Quantity limits provision
    - ▪ Predatory pricing
- The Fair Packaging and Labeling Act (The Hart Act) (1966)
  - o Altered the way products are packaged
  - o Requires that a label state the identity of the product, the net quantity of the contents, and the name and place of business of the manufacturer or distributor
  - o The act sought to eliminate misleading descriptions and illustrations and to force companies to adopt standard packaging sizes
- Package Label Regulations
  - o The federal government requires the labels of packaged, processed foods to contain the following information:
    - ▪ The common or legal name of the product
    - ▪ The name and address of the food processor, or the distributor of the items
    - ▪ The net contents in the package, listed according to count, weight, or other appropriate measure
    - ▪ A listing of ingredients in descending order, from greatest proportion to least proportion
    - ▪ A notation of any artificial flavoring or chemical preservatives added to the product
    - ▪ Serving size and number of servings per container
    - ▪ Number of calories per serving
    - ▪ Number of calories derived from fat
    - ▪ Amounts of fat, saturated fat, cholesterol, sodium, sugars, dietary fiber, protein, total carbohydrates, and complex carbohydrates
    - ▪ Amounts of important vitamins and minerals
    - ▪ If the product is a beverage, the amount of juice it contains
    - ▪ A notation that the product falls below the standard of fill, if relevant

- All label information must be noted in English unless an imported product with a foreign-language will not deceive customers, or if such a product will be distributed in an area where the foreign language is the predominant language
  - If the food processor makes any nutritional or dietary claims, the package must carry government-approved terminology
  - A standardized list of nutrient facts, as articulated by the Nutrition Labeling and Education Act
  - If the product is raw or partially cooked meat or poultry, it must contain safe-handling instructions on the label
- Franchise Law
  - A franchisor can legally require franchisees to adhere to specific standards of quality
  - Usually a franchisor will not force a franchisee to purchase from the franchisor's commissary and/or central distribution center, nor would a franchisee necessarily be required to buy from a supplier designated by the franchisor
- The Internal Revenue Service and the Bureau of Alcohol, Tobacco, and Firearms
  - The Internal Revenue Service and the Bureau of Alcohol, Tobacco, and Firearms are responsible for the orderly and legal sale, distribution and purchase of alcoholic beverages
  - These agencies ensure that:
    - No adulterated product enters the marketplace
    - Products are produced, sold, distributed and purchased by duly licensed entities only
    - All applicable taxes and fees are collected
- State and local legislation
  - Some states and municipalities have adopted somewhat stricter versions of the federal laws, as well as some not found in federal statutes
- Contract law
  - Contract: a voluntary and lawful agreement, by competent parties, for a good consideration, to do or not do a specified thing
  - A completed purchase order, accepted by a supplier, becomes a legally enforceable contract.
  - A verbal commitment can carry the force of a written contract
  - Technically, no contract exists if a supplier does not acknowledge his or her intent to enter into a legally binding agreement
  - Once goods are delivered, the buyer will deem them acceptable and will pay for the merchandise
    - Legal problems might arise if the goods delivered do not meet the agreed-upon standards of quality, quantity, and price
    - A buyer is able to return these goods upon:
      - Inspecting a representative sample of the goods
      - Indicating why the goods are not acceptable
      - Informing the supplier that the goods are being rejected
- Agency law
  - Salespersons need to know the precise authority operators delegate to their buyers
  - Buyers have the authority, as their company's agents, to legally bind their companies to purchase order contracts
    - Hospitality companies usually limit a buyer's authority by setting a dollar limit on the purchases he or she can contract for
    - If such a limitation exists, salespersons and their companies must be notified

- Title to goods
  - It is important for buyers to know the precise moment when title to any product passes to their firm
    - At the point of title transfer, the buyer's firm assumes responsibility for the item
    - Title can pass at any one of many points in the market channel
    - When purchasing from intermediaries, the hospitality operation takes title when a receiving agent receives, inspects, and signs for the delivered merchandise
    - Under a direct-buying arrangement, the hospitality operation takes title when the merchandise leaves the primary source's premises
    - If the buyer takes title before actually receiving the item, it, as well as the risk, belongs to that company
- Consignment sales
  - Consignment sales are not common in the hospitality industry, and are not allowed for alcoholic beverages
    - They do appear now and then , especially in seasonal resort areas
    - Off-premise caterers tend to rely on consignment sales from time to time
  - A typical consignment sale stipulates that the buyer of a product need not pay until the acquiring company sells the product
- Warranties and Guarantees
  - Warranties and guarantees may be either "expressed" or "implied"
    - Express warranty/guarantee: written out in straightforward language
    - Implied warranty/guarantees: either inferred by the buyer or implied by the seller
  - Courts of law allow salespersons to voice a degree of prideful exaggeration about their products
    - A buyer may face problems if seeking retribution when the product is not "the best in the land"
- Patents
  - Retailers must be careful to avoid illegally adopting someone else's patented procedures
  - Copyrights cannot be violated
- Rebates
  - Rebates, which are gifts of cash or product, are legal as long as suppliers offer all buyers the same rebate possibility
  - An exception exists in the liquor trade, in which all rebates are illegal on the wholesale level
  - A buyer could be unknowingly implicated in a legal action if he or she takes a rebate, assuming that all other buyers have had the same opportunity, when in fact he or she is the only buyer receiving the rebate
  - Rebates are also against the law when a buyer and seller conspire to inflate the price of a product and the buyer takes a personal rebate after the purchase
6. Technological force
  - Many technological advances in the hospitality channel of distribution have taken place
  - Genetically engineered foods
  - Product preservation
  - Value-added foods
    - While it is generally true that a value-added food is much more expensive than its raw counterpart, the potential savings in labor preparation time, energy usage, and storing and handling chores may reduce the EP cost to the point at which overall profit margins will be attractive

- In some cases, the AP price of a convenience food may actually be less than the AP price of the raw ingredients needed to fabricate the item
- Today, almost every food item has some degree of form value added to it
- Transportation
  - In many respects, faster transportation constitutes a form of product preservation
    - Buyers can expect faster, larger, and more predictable deliveries, reducing the number of purchase orders buyers must make
    - The increased dependability of transportation allows the buyer to fulfill more readily the promises they make to their customers
- Computerization
- Packaging
  - According to the USDA, packaging accounts for about 8 percent of the purchase price of food products
  - The USDA also estimates that in about one-fourth of all food and beverages sold, packaging costs exceed the cost of edible ingredients
  - Directly affects the quality, shelf life, and convenience of the food or beverage products
  - Some packaging can contribute to better taste
    - Many products are packed in controlled atmosphere packaging (CAP)
    - Some common forms of CAP – also referred to as modified atmosphere packaging (MAP) are the aseptic packs that are used to package juices, wines, and unrefrigerated milk; shelf stable, unrefrigerated convenience meals; and processed produce and other grocery products
    - A packaging advance is the application if the Universal Product Code (UPC)
      - Use of this technology will lead to more efficient order processing, improved receiving operations, more accurate inventory valuation and control, and increased opportunities to do business electronically

7. Other forces
   - It may be more appropriate to label other forces "intangible forces"
   - Such factors as a supplier's advertising and promotion effectiveness, pricing policy, credit terms, and the conviviality of salespersons fall within this category and certainly affect the channel of distribution

True/False

T F 1. The Pure Food Act and the Federal Meat Inspection Act were both passed in 1906 as a result of Upton Sinclair's book *The Jungle*.

T F 2. Rebates, which are gifts of cash or product, are legal as long as they are restricted to a certain group of buyers and not offered to everyone.

T F 3. Before the Poultry Products Inspection Act was passed in 1957, all poultry inspections were conducted on a voluntary basis.

T F 4. There is no clear-cut definition of ethical behavior though the Institute for Supply Management and the International Society of Hospitality Purchasers (ISHP) have both developed codes of ethics to guide members.

T F 5. Pesticide residuals in foods were regulated by the Food Quality Protection ACT (FQPA) which was passed in 1996.

T F 6. It takes more time for the Food and Drug Administration (FDA) to recall products than any other agency.

T F 7. If a buyer takes title to an item before actually receiving it (or perhaps before even paying for it), the buyer may have to pay a higher AP price.

T F 8. A consignment sale is one where the buyer of a product need not pay until he/she sells the product.

T F 9. An agreement must be in writing for it to be legally enforceable.

T F 10. A franchisor can legally require that franchisees adhere to certain standards of quality.

Fill-in-the-Blank

1. Antitrust legislation has had a tremendous impact on supply channel activities. The _____ was passed in 1890 to forbid any action that restricted or eliminated competition in the marketplace. The _____ was established in 1914 to deal with advertising or promotion deceptions, and monopolies. It was amended by the Wheeler-Lea Act in 1938. The _____, also passed in 1914, was yet another effort to increase the government's control over antitrust activities. This act defined the antitrust duties of the FTC.

2. Ralph Nader was a consumer activist who led a group called "Nader's Raiders." In 1967 his activities focusing on continuing abuses in the meat industry resulted in the passage of _____. Other related meat safety acts include the Poultry Products Inspection Act, passed in 1957, and the _____ passed in 1968.

3. An _____ warranty or guarantee is a written document whereas a _____ warranty or guarantee is a verbal agreement.

4. Transporting a product across state lines constitutes interstate commerce. The _____ was passed in 1930 to prohibit fraudulent practices in the sale of fresh and frozen produce.

5. Two activities are specifically prohibited by the Clayton Act of 1914. These include _____ where a buyer is forced to buy certain products to have the "right" to purchase other, perhaps more necessary products and _____ where a supplier forces a buyer to use only his or her products.

6. The _____ was established to enforce the laws and regulations covered in the Federal Food, Drug and Cosmetic Act.

7. The Fair Packaging and Labeling Act, also known as the _____, did much to change the "look" of today's products, but failed to succeed in forcing companies to adopt standard packaging sizes.

8. The _____, passed in 1992 stipulates, among other things, that only tuna that is harvested without harming dolphins may be sold.

9. Two types of packaging where a vacuum is created around the product and a special mixture of gases is added are known as _____ and _____.

10. The Robinson-Patman Act specifically addressed and made illegal which three supplier practices?
   _____, _____, _____

Multiple Choice

1. A Pathogen Reduction/Hazard Analysis Critical Control Points (HACCP) Rule, which requires food processors to identify critical points within the production where foods could become contaminated, was added in 1996 to which acts?
   a. Clayton Act and the Agricultural Adjustment Act
   b. Wholesome Meat Act and the Robinson-Patman Act
   c. Clayton Act and the Wholesome Poultry Products Act
   d. Wholesome Meat Act and the Wholesome Poultry Products Act

2. Which of the following deals with unlawful activities in the marketplace including antitrust violations?
   a. USDA
   b. FTC
   c. FDA
   d. NOAA

3. Passed in 1906, the Federal Food, Drug and Cosmetic Act covers which of the following?
   a. random inspections of home kitchens
   b. random inspections of meat processors
   c. random inspections of food-processing plants
   d. random inspections of drug stores

4. The Fair Packaging and Labeling Act includes all of the following except:
   a. serving size
   b. common or legal name of the product
   c. price
   d. nutrition facts

5. Which of the following is not a method of preserving foods?
   a. irradiation
   b. genetic engineering
   c. government-approved hormones
   d. chemical preservatives

6. Which of the following is not a step in the return of goods?
   a. inspecting a representative sample
   b. finding out the goods can be purchased more cheaply elsewhere
   c. indicating the problem with the goods
   d. informing the supplier that the goods are being rejected

7. Packaging accounts for as much as 8 percent of the purchase price of a product. However, new packaging processes are helping preserve food, improve the taste and even increase the safety. Which of the following is not an advantage of the aseptic pack?
   a. stacks readily and take up less space than conventional packaging
   b. cheaper than conventional packaging
   c. increases food safety with time- and temperature-sensitive labels
   d. does not require refrigerated storage

8. A salesperson's personality and a supplier's pricing policy are examples of which factor affecting the distribution system?
    a. economic force
    b. legal restrictions
    c. intangible force
    d. technological advances

9. Which of the following was not specifically developed to reduce product spoilage?
    a. irradiation techniques
    b. controlled atmosphere packaging
    c. genetically engineered foods
    d. convenience foods

10. Which of the following is true?
    a. there is a great distinction between the same quality of wheat grown on one farm versus another
    b. supply and demand have very little effect on the distribution system
    c. adding value to a product is one way to differentiate it from other similar products in the marketplace
    d. prices are usually the same for products with similar qualities

Apply Your Knowledge
1. Discuss the requirements and regulations for food processing safety, handling and labeling from a buyer's perspective. Do these political forces help or hinder the distribution system?

2. Genetically altered and irradiated foods, may last longer but they are not always popular with customers. Discuss your feelings about using these products in your operation and how forthcoming your employees should be with this information when asked by a customer, "Were these tomatoes irradiated? I don't eat irradiated foods."

3. Discus the concept of monopolistic competition and explain how it pertains to the forces affecting the distribution system.

Chapter 5
An Overview of the Purchasing Function
After reading this chapter, you should be able to:
- Describe the purchasing activities in a hospitality operation.
- Determine the purchasing requirements of a hospitality operation using value analysis and make-or-buy analysis.
- Outline the objectives of the purchasing function and the potential problems that buyers encounter when pursuing those objectives.

Outline
1. Introduction
    - All hospitality operations, no matter how large or small, have purchasing activities in common
    - The difference between a large and small operation is how much time and attention these activities receive
2. Purchasing Activities
    - Common purchasing activities
        o Determine when to order
        o Control inventory levels
        o Establish quality standards
        o Determine specifications
        o Obtain competitive bids
        o Investigate vendors
        o Arrange financial terms
        o Oversee delivery
        o Negotiate refunds
        o Handle adjustments
        o Arrange for storage
    - Foodservice purchasing activities
        o Recipe development
        o Menu development
        o Specification writing
        o Approval of buying source
        o Designation of approved brands
        o Supplier evaluation
        o Negotiation with suppliers
        o Change of suppliers
        o Change of brands
        o Substitution of approved items
        o Approval of new products
        o Invoice approval
        o Invoice payment
        o Order placement with supplier
    - Selection and procurement plan
        o How organization intends to select/procure products and services
        o Outline of supplier availability
        o Purchasing trends
        o Procedure for revising the plan
    - Determine requirements
        o Determine varieties and amounts of products, services, equipment and furnishings needed by the operation

- o Work with other managers, end users of the products
- Supplier selection
- Sourcing
  - o When a buyer establishers a supplier, it is called "sourcing"
  - o Usually happens when buyer is seeking specific or hard-to-find product
- Maintain a convenient and sufficient inventory
  - o Optimal inventory management
    - Too small will result in stockouts
    - Too large ties up unnecessary dollars in inventory and storage costs
- Conduct negotiations
- Research activities
  - o Value analysis
    - Examining a product to identify unnecessary costs that can be cut without sacrificing quality or performance
    - Goal is to increase value by manipulating quality, supplier services and edible-portion costs
    - No purchasing change should be made without consulting end user of product under study
  - o Forecasting
    - Predicting the kinds of products and services that will be available in the future and their prices
    - Can now be tracked online: National Restaurant Association restaurant trendmapper (http://www.restaurant.org/trendmapper)
  - o What-if analysis
    - What if the price of one product goes, what happens to the overall food cost as a result
    - Increase in overall food cost = percentage price increase for the ingredient x the ingredient's percentage of overall food cost
  - o Make-or-buy analysis
    - Value-added products offer many advantages
      - Consistent quality
      - Consistent portion control
      - Opportunity to serve diverse menu regardless of skill level
      - Operating efficiencies (less energy to reconstitute than prepare from scratch)
      - Less food-handler supervision
      - Reduced employee skill requirements
      - Reduction in leftovers
      - Reduction of raw-materials inventory
      - Reduction in ordering costs (ordering one product not multiple ingredients)
      - Increase in edible yields
      - Possible reduction in size and storage needs of kitchen facility
    - Disadvantage of value-added products is high cost
    - Making a product in-house or purchasing it ready-made requires consideration of numerous factors
  - o Plant visits
- Maintain supplier diplomacy
  - o Trade Relations – spreading the purchasing dollar among as many suppliers as possible

- Educate suppliers
  - Keeping suppliers informed of changing needs so they can plan accordingly
  - Taking the time to "pick the brains" of suppliers to stay current with trends and maintain knowledge of changing hospitality market
- Purchase, receive, store and issue products
- Disposal of excess and unsalable items
- Recycling
- Develop record-keeping controls
  - Maintain record of product as it moves through the organization
- Organize and administer the purchasing function
- Self-improvement
  - Association meetings, seminars, trade show visits, continuing education
  - Certifications: Certified Purchasing Manager (CPM); Accredited Purchasing Practitioner (APP)
- Help competitors
  - You help them in an emergency, they'll help you
  - Learn more about hospitality market through talking with peers
- Other activities

3. Purchasing Objectives
  - Maintain an adequate supply
  - Minimize investment
  - Maintain quality
  - Obtain the lowest possible EP cost
  - Maintain the company's competitive position

4. Problems of the Buyer
  - Backdoor selling where a supplier presents new products to other employees, hoping they will request that the new products be purchases
  - Developing optimum amount of time to spend with suppliers
  - Ethical traps
  - Buyer may have responsibility for purchasing, but not the authority to act accordingly
  - Buyer may have responsibility for purchasing, but not the time to do the job right
  - Buyer may find it difficult to work with other department heads and managers
  - Department heads and managers may make unreasonable demands of buyers
  - Late deliveries and related problems with receiving and storage can undermine efficient purchasing plan
  - Failure on the part of management and others to recognize purchasing as a profit-making activity
  - Suppliers may be out of products, sending unacceptable substitutes instead
  - Suppliers may not be interested in buyer's business, especially if he is a "small stop"
  - Receiving and storage inadequacies may make it difficult to protect the merchandise after it is delivered
  - Suppliers may be out of products and may note that the items are "back ordered" and will be shipped at a later date
  - Returns and allowances will happen because some merchandise will be unusable for one reason or another

5. Evaluation of the Purchasing Function
  - Balancing costs of a buyer's salary and receiving and inventory management with the less evident benefits can be challenging
  - In authors' opinion, the benefits outweigh the costs

True/False

T F 1.   Buyer's activities differ dramatically from one hospitality operation to another depending on the size of the organization.

T F 2.   The Institute of Supply Management offers two levels of certifications for buyers, the Certified Purchasing Manager (CPM) and the Accredited Purchasing Practitioner (APP).

T F 3.   Minimizing a company's investment in inventory while at the same time, maintaining adequate supplies is very challenging for buyers.

T F 4.   Negotiating power is based strictly on the relationship a buyer has developed with the supplier and has nothing to do with the money the buyer expects to spend.

T F 5.   The task of developing specifications does not always fall on the shoulders of the buyer. He or she may get input from managers, consultants or others.

T F 6.   The AP price is the only factor the buyer needs to consider; the EP cost is really only relevant for the chefs in the kitchen.

T F 7.   Tracking returned products and ensuring that the proper credit is given on the supplier's bills is one of a buyer's challenges.

T F 8.   As companies downsize, buyers may find themselves responsible for more than the purchasing function.

T F 9.   Lending product to a competitor is a good practice that helps establish a reciprocal arrangement where you could in turn ask to borrow something in an emergency.

T F 10. Sometimes a buyer becomes a seller when he or she is tasked with getting rid of obsolete, overstocked or unnecessary items.

Fill-in-the-Blank

1.   Sometimes suppliers are looking for help with the sales effort. They will go to people other than the buyer to pitch products. For example, a supplier might visit with the head of housekeeping and tout the value of a new cleanser, hoping that he or she will ask the buyer to purchase the new product. This practice on the part of the supplier is known as _____.

2.   _____ and _____ are two related terms that describe the activities of seeking out and enlisting the services of a supplier for one or more products.

3.   Buyers need to be constantly researching possible substitutes for the products they purchase in an effort to eliminate unnecessary costs. Think of the process that Danny Campbell went through when trying to determine whether a different, less expensive napkin for the buffet might serve the Silverton Casino Lodge just as well as the current napkin (Chapter 1). This process is known as _____.

4.   Buyers are often asked to determine whether it would be better to purchase a prepared product or make it in-house instead. This analysis is known as _____. There are many advantages to convenience foods, but the main disadvantage is _____.

5.	Purchasing the majority of one's products from a single supplier is known as _____.
The opposite of this practice is known as _____ and is where a company spreads
purchase dollars among as many suppliers as possible.

6.	Purchasers often find themselves needing to predict which products are going to be available in the
future and in what quantities at what cost. This is known as _____. This process is
particularly important when creating budgets for the coming year. Another analysis, known as the
_____, helps a buyer determine the impact a change in price of an item will have on the
bottom line.

7.	Through the North American Association of Food Equipment Manufacturers (NAFEM), one can
become a _____. This certification is for those purchasing professionals who specialize
in equipment purchasing.

8.	When a product that has been ordered is not available, a supplier may indicate that it is on
_____ and will be available at a later date.

9.	It is a buyer's goal to _____ inventory while _____ the company's
inventory investment.

10.	A buyer who does not make large purchases may be known to the supplier as a _____
and may not receive the same service and attention as a buyer for a larger operation.

Multiple Choice
1.	Which of the items below is not an advantage of convenience or prepared products?
	a. consistent portion control
	b. consistent quality
	c. high-level employee skill requirements
	d. reduction of raw-materials inventory

2.	A buyer is likely to be most challenged by which of the following?
	a. lack of general suppliers to choose from
	b. too much buying authority
	c. suppliers who often substitute items or place products on back order
	d. lack of product information

3.	Foodservice purchasing activities might include all of the following except:
	a. approval of buying sources
	b. recipe development
	c. invoice payment
	d. management of waitstaff

4.	An optimal inventory is one that:
	a. minimizes stockouts
	b. optimizes the company's investment in food items and supplies
	c. includes items "a" and "b" above
	d. includes none of the above

5. All of the following are purchasing activities except:
   a. conducting negotiations with suppliers
   b. educating suppliers
   c. continuing to study and learn (self-improvement)
   d. all are purchasing activities

6. If the price of butter is expected to increase 30% and butter is 5% of the overall food budget, what will be the effect on the coming year's food costs?
   a. increase 15%
   b. increase 1.5%
   c. increase .015%
   d. little or no change

7. A buyer who was being hounded by employees to purchase products new on the market might suspect that his or her supplier was doing which of the following?
   a. backdoor selling
   b. back ordering
   c. wasting time on a small stop
   d. taking up too much of his or her time

8. Obtaining the lowest possible edible portion cost is one of the objectives of purchasing. Which of the following activities would contribute the least toward achieving this goal?
   a. conducting a make-or-buy analysis
   b. conducting a value analysis
   c. conducting a what-if analysis
   d. making plant visits

9. How could a buyer's failure to properly receive and store products lead to a higher than usual EP cost?
   a. products could spoil and become unusable
   b. products might be stolen off the loading dock or out of the storeroom
   c. "a" and "b" above
   d. none of the above

10. A buyer who is working in an atmosphere of rising butter prices might conduct a what-if analysis. He would want to share his results with which of the following persons?
    a. head chef before he plans menus for the coming quarter
    b. accounting department head
    c. owner/manager
    d. all of the above

Apply Your Knowledge

1. Think of a buyer's relationship with his or her suppliers. How many of the 14 problems of the buyer relate to this relationship and how might you overcome these issues as you negotiate contracts and choose supplier services?

2. Your manager doesn't see the value of all of the time you spend conducting value analyses and doing other research. Explain how these activities directly affect the company's bottom line.

3. Imagine that you are a busy buyer and trying to set some guidelines for supplier visits to your office. Think through what you would learn or gain from such a visit and decide how often and how long you should make yourself available for supplier contact.

Chapter 6
The Organization and Administration of Purchasing
After reading this chapter, you should be able to:
- Describe the methods used to plan and organize the purchasing activities of a hospitality operator.
- Recognize the issues involved in administering the purchasing activities of a hospitality operator.

Outline
1. Introduction—buyers must plan, organize and administer the purchasing activities
2. Planning
   - Important to understand the objectives of purchasing
     - Maintain adequate supply
     - Minimize investment
     - Maintain quality
     - Obtain lowest possible edible-portion (EP) cost
     - Maintain competitive advantage
   - Selecting from many methods to achieve these objectives is main part of planning
   - Initial planning decisions set the stage for all future activities
   - Involve middle and upper managers
     - Provide list of objectives of purchasing, ask for information on how they might affect their area of operation
     - Schedule a meeting for discussion
   - Organizing—process of organizing the human and material resources to follow the plan
     - Organizational pattern for the independent operator
     - Organizational pattern for the multi-unit chain operations
   - Organizing for the independent operation
     - Small "mom and pop" organizations
       - Selection and procurement responsibilities of owner-manager
       - Hourly employees involved in purchasing activities on rare occasions
     - Medium independents
       - Rarely have full-time buyers, utilize user-buyer system
       - Owner-manager coordinates buying activities and oversees receiving, storing and bill-paying
       - In some cases, steward or assistant manager may coordinate user-buyers
       - Steward may sometimes work specifically as buyer in the kitchen and oversee warewashing and the kitchen cleaning employees
     - Communal buying, co-op purchasing, shared buying
       - Utilized mostly by small and medium independents
       - Lower AP prices for larger orders
       - Works for food, operating supplies, insurance, advertising and other purchases
       - Owner-managers share the task of coordinating orders or, as a group, may hire someone to perform this task
     - Large independents
       - Have one or more persons assigned to purchasing, receiving, storing and issuing of products or services
       - Usually have purchasing director with specialists in buying food, beverages and equipment/supplies
       - Receiving clerk might work for accounting department and storeroom manager for the purchasing department

- Organizing for chain operations—similar to large independents, but has added level of management, usually a vice president of purchasing or corporate purchasing director and a staff of buyers
  - Local unit level
    - Sometimes unit manager does all buying or perhaps serves as coordinator for user-buyers
    - Franchisee
      - Buys from suppliers approved by corporate
      - Buys from other suppliers that meet corporate standards
      - Buys from company-owned commissary or central distribution center
      - Uses a combination of all three of the above
    - Company-owned stores
      - Managers have same options as above but less flexibility
  - Vice president of purchasing
    - Sets purchasing guidelines
    - Negotiates national, long-term contracts
    - Sets purchase specifications
    - Performs research activities
    - Serves as a resource person for unit managers and unit buying personnel
    - Supervises central distribution function or commissary if applicable
  - Centralized purchasing
    - Advantage—lower AP prices achieved by quantity buys and presence of a strong negotiator
    - Disadvantage—alienation of local suppliers; company not seen as good community citizen
    - Some decentralization inevitable
      - VP of purchasing can't purchase nor negotiate contracts for everything
      - Soothes feelings of local suppliers
      - Gives unit personnel purchasing experience
3. Staffing
   - Small and medium operations usually don't have full-time buyers
   - Large operations
     - Several specialized buyers
     - Secretarial or clerical personnel
     - Receiving clerks and storeroom managers
   - Job Specifications
     - Technical
     - Conceptual
     - Human
4. Training
   - Entry level
     - Job and company orientation
     - Formal instruction
     - On-the-job training
   - Training Options
     - National Restaurant Association (NRA)
     - National Restaurant Association Educational Foundation (NRAEF)
     - Institute of Supply Management (ISM)
     - North American Association of Food Equipment Manufacturers (NAFEM)

5. Budgeting—operations with full-time buyers will need to budget the purchasing function with buyers' and clerical employees' salaries and benefits
6. Directing—buyers must supervise the purchasing personnel assigned to them
7. Controlling

True/False

T F 1. The five purchasing objectives can be used as a foundation when developing a procurement plan.

T F 2. Middle and upper managers should not be involved in the planning process—they have too many ideas and will only slow things down.

T F 3. In small operations, people often have to fill several roles. For example, one might not only be the chef, but the user-buyer for the kitchen as well.

T F 4. You can learn more about cooperative purchasing at www.ncba.coop, the website of the National Cooperative Business Association (NCBA).

T F 5. In a large operation, one might find separate buyers specializing in food, beverages, or equipment and supplies.

T F 6. A buyer's performance may be evaluated based on a comparison of actual expenditures with the budgeted expenses.

T F 7. The owner-manager should feel quite confident to turn over the purchasing responsibilities to an employee with little or no supervision.

T F 8. A local buyer in a multi-unit chain operation with a commissary has more decision-making power than a buyer in a medium-size independent company.

T F 9. In a large operation, the control function may be covered, in part, with a series of paper and computerized forms.

T F 10. One or more persons serving the buying function is typical of a small independent operation.

Fill-in-the-Blank

1. Staffing, training, and budgeting are examples of activity areas that must be examined in the purchasing organization. _____ is a broad term which covers such tasks as the tracking and security of products once they arrive on property; ensuring that purchasers at different properties are using preferred vendors, and working to eliminate waste and spoilage.

2. A _____ system is one in which the owner-manager keeps an eye on all purchasing operations. This is almost the opposite of the _____ system which utilizes computerized and/or paper forms to keep track of products once on the property.

3. Communal buying is also known as _____ or _____.

4. One who is responsible for purchasing the items he or she uses is known as a _____. This type of buying arrangement would most likely be found in a _____ type of operation.

5. In a multi-unit chain operation, a _____ who would be in the corporate office, has a number of tasks including negotiating contracts, developing purchase specifications and identifying _____ or those sources that local managers can use because they meet company standard.

Multiple Choice

1. Which of the following is usually not an option for a unit manager?
   a. to buy from approved suppliers
   b. to buy from the commissary
   c. to buy from any suppliers found on the Internet
   d. to buy from local suppliers that meet company standards

2. If the owner of a small independent decides that the lowest AP price is the basis for her purchasing plan, she will probably do which of the following:
   a. continually shop around for new suppliers
   b. ask for extra supplier services
   c. buy exclusively from one supplier
   d. be inflexible about delivery schedules and payment terms

3. Budgeting, directing and controlling are three activities of
   a. planning for the purchasing function
   b. administering the purchasing function
   c. organizing the purchasing function
   d. none of the above

4. The purchasing responsibilities of a manager of a franchise operation differs from that of a company-owned operation in what way?
   a. franchisee has more items to order
   b. franchisee has more buyers to supervise
   c. franchisee has more flexibility
   d. franchisee may make purchases from the commissary

5. Training for an entry-level buyer might include all of the following except:
   a. introduction to company goals and objectives
   b. shadowing of various employees to learn their jobs and how they use different products
   c. formal instruction
   d. cooking school

Apply Your Knowledge

1. Look at the goals and objectives of the purchasing function and discuss how each could contribute to an overall purchasing plan.

2. Discuss how waste, spoilage and security issues complicate a buyer's responsibility for control over products.

3. Think about a hospitality operation's role as a community "citizen." In addition to purchasing from local suppliers, what other ways might a company model good citizenship?

Chapter 7
The Buyer's Relations with Other Company Personnel

After reading this chapter, you should be able to:

- Describe the buyer's relationship with others in the hospitality organization.
- Explain various methods used to evaluate a buyer's performance.

Outline

1. Introduction
   - Buyer and owner-manager are often the same
   - Large operations have part-time or full-time buyers
     - o Some organizations have full-time buyer and department heads that make specialized purchases
   - Multi-unit organizations often have corporate purchasing agent with a buyer or buyer-manager at each location
   - Full-time buyer is a member of management
     - o Exercises line authority over designated purchasing functions
     - o Sometimes supervises other staff members
2. The Buyer's Relations with the Supervisor
   - The job specification
     - o Lists the qualities sought in a job candidate
       - ▪ Technical skill
         - Familiarity with all items purchased
         - Knowledge of how items will be used
       - ▪ Interpersonal (or human) skill
         - Must be able to get along with others
         - Must be able to be firm but fair with suppliers
       - ▪ Conceptual skill
         - Ability to view operation as a whole, not just from the vantage point of the purchasing department
         - Helps to have a "systems" mentality
       - ▪ Other qualities
         - Quality and types of an applicant's experience
         - Honesty and integrity
         - Desire to advance and grow with the operation
         - Ability to administer a purchasing department
         - Desire to work conscientiously for the operation
   - Labor pool
     - o Finding a full-time buyer
       - ▪ Moving/promoting an existing employee
       - ▪ Newspaper or other advertising
       - ▪ Inquiring among friends or colleagues
     - o Finding a part-time buyer
       - ▪ Same methods as for full-time buyer
       - ▪ One challenge – how much emphasis do you put on the "purchasing" portion of a job for a chef who is also going to do the buying for the kitchen
   - Budgeting
     - o Large operations may fund purchasing
       - ▪ Salaries
       - ▪ Operating expenses

- o Buyer's performance can be measured by comparing actual with budgeted operating expenses
- Job description
  - o List of duties an employee must perform
- Objectives of the purchasing function
  - o Standard objectives
    - Purchasing appropriate quality
    - Purchasing at the right price
    - Purchasing in the right amount
    - Purchasing at the right time
    - Purchasing from the right supplier
  - o Some organizations may have additional, more rigid standards regarding quality or other company guidelines
- Selection and procurement policies
  - o Accepting gifts from a supplier
    - Strict rules against this practice are the norm
    - Taking gifts may set up a psychological obligation to purchase goods from the gift-giving supplier
  - o Favoring supplier
    - Buyers are sometimes given an approved supplier list
    - Not a good practice to buy exclusively from a relative or friend
  - o Limiting quantity
    - Usually there are limits on amount buyer may purchase at one time to avoid overstocks, storage issues and hindered cash flow because funds are tied up in inventory
  - o Limiting prices
    - Buyers usually have flexible price limits
    - Items that rise above those limits bear watching
  - o Making personal purchases
    - Steward sales – when company allows employees to take advantage of its buying power to purchase goods for private use
    - Often happens at holiday time
  - o Establishing reciprocity
    - You buy from me, I'll buy from you
    - At best, a buyer will break even
    - Buyer purchases more from supplier than supplier could ever refer food business
  - o Accepting free samples
    - Buyer should limit this to time when he or she is serious about purchasing the product
    - Free equipment testing falls in the same guidelines
    - Difficulty is when company sends most expensive items and then pressures buyer to purchase them
  - o Accepting discounts
    - Quantity discount: buyer agrees to purchase a large amount of one specific type of merchandise
    - Volume discount: buyer agrees to purchase a large volume of a number of different items; often referred to as a "blanket discount"
    - Cash Discount: award for prompt payment, payment in advance of the delivery or using a cash-on-delivery (COD) system

- Promotional discount: a buyer might agree to promote a certain product carried by the supplier and the supplier will provide the product and perhaps even promotional materials at a reduced cost
  - Some companies seek this type of discount
  - Others are concerned about tying themselves to a specific product
- Following the written code of ethics
- Controlling products
  - Buyer may be responsible for receiving, storage and use of products
  - Receiving clerk often employee of receiving department; each division of labor provides more control as people check on each other's performance
- Supporting local suppliers
- Adhering to quality standards
- Following shopping procedures
  - Set procedures for selecting the appropriate supplier
  - Buyer offering best value is found by shopping around
- Compensation
  - Buyers are usually on salary, but some receive a bonus
  - Corporate purchasing agents get a good salary and are part of the top management team
  - Bonuses are tricky to assign-what may bring about the highest bonus for the buyer may not be in the company's best interest
- Training
- Performance evaluation
  - How well the purchasing department is operated
  - How well the procurement function is carried out
  - Operational performance is how well the buyer has adhered to the budget allocated for the purchasing department (salaries, office supplies, etc.)
  - The materials budget
    - Based on the goods sold, as an example, food costs might be estimated at 35 percent of the food-sales dollar
    - Easy to compare actual costs with budgeted for a procurement performance evaluation
    - This type of budget occurs mainly in hospitality organizations serving captive audiences (schools, prison food services, etc.)
- Inventory turnover
  - Calculated by dividing the annual cost of goods sold by the average dollar value of inventory
  - Average dollar value of inventory equals the beginning inventory plus the ending inventory divided by 2
  - Normal food turnover is 20 to 25 times a year (about two weeks for food items to move from the receiving dock to a customer's stomach)
- Percentage of sales volume
  - Food operation should have an inventory of food, beverage and nonfood supplies equal to no more than 1 percent of annual sales
  - Another rule of thumb: food inventory should be no more than about one-third of the annual monthly food costs
- Stockouts
- Number of late deliveries
- Number of items that must be returned to suppliers
- Number of back orders

- Checking AP prices
  - Supervisors should check AP prices of other suppliers on a regular basis and comparing it with those of current suppliers
  - Helps keep buyers from taking tempting kickbacks from suppliers
- Other performance indicators
  - Wise supervisors establish clearly defined and easily measured goals
  - Buyers should be evaluated on:
    - Number of stockouts
    - Inventory stock levels
    - Percentage of returns
    - Losses due to overbuying
    - Losses due to user's refusal of an item
    - Inventory turnover
  - Another issue—how to evaluate the part-time buyer
- Other relations between buyers and supervisors
  - Supervisors expect buyers to
    - Give pertinent advice when necessary
    - Be loyal to the company
    - Put the company's interests ahead of personal interests
    - Maintain good working relationships with suppliers and company personnel
    - Remember that he or she is a representative of the company in the marketplace
    - Avoid legal entanglements
    - Avoid favoritism or discrimination when dealing with suppliers
  - Buyers expect supervisors to
    - Give them the authority perform the job
    - Give them adequate facilities and budget
    - Give them a voice in major decisions
    - Have an appreciation of the profit potential of the buying activity
3. The Buyer's Relations with Colleagues
   - Should strive to help each other
     - Housekeeping user-buyer may agree to buy cleaning supplies for everyone
     - Buyer-chef may need to work with accountant to develop ordering, receiving protocol
   - Potential conflicts with colleagues
     - Buyer may work hard to obtain lowest possible EP cost, but might find waste in the kitchen
     - Chef may blame higher than usual EP cost on buyer's purchase of inferior merchandise
     - Some organizations minimize these problems by having a buyer-chef, a buyer-head bartender, etc.
4. The Buyer's Relations with Hourly Employees
   - Buyer's responsibility to hourly employees is to provide the resources need to carry out their duties; buyer must ensure a continuity of supply
   - Buyer will be responsible for steward sales
   - Potential conflicts with hourly employees arise if buyer tries to exert too much control over employees someone else supervises

True/False

T F 1. The quality indicators for procurement performance have been standardized throughout the industry.

T F 2. Too many late deliveries may be reason to change suppliers.

T F 3. Because they know what is available, buyers often have the final say as to the quality of the products they are ordering.

T F 4. A receiving clerk who reports to the accounting department rather than purchasing is a good check on the activities of the buyer, a control on his or her purchases.

T F 5. Whether to accept free samples is one of the many ethical decisions a buyer must make every day.

T F 6. Job descriptions and job specifications are essentially the same things.

T F 7. The ending inventory of one month becomes the beginning inventory of the following month.

T F 8. The list of a company's acceptable suppliers is known as the labor pool.

T F 9. The normal turnover for liquor is between 7 and 10 times a year.

T F 10. Accepting gifts from suppliers is not only considered to be unethical, it can create a psychological obligation to purchase from that supplier.

Fill-in-the-Blank

1. Maintaining a balance between having too much inventory and not enough inventory is a continuous balancing act for most companies. A _____ is the result of a supplier not having a requested product. A _____ is when a hotel or restaurant is out of a needed item.

2. Let's say a supplier spends time visiting with the chef about a new convenience food product that would cut down on the time she spends creating sauces. The supplier's hope is that the chef will request that this product be purchased. This practice on the part of the supplier is known as _____ .

3. There are three basic skills a good buyer should possess. _____ allow the buyer to see the big picture of the hospitality operation. With _____ , a buyer is able to relate to other people in the organization and interact firmly and fairly with buyers. A buyer with strong _____ has a good understanding of how all of the products are used by employees within the organization.

4. _____ is the term for a relationship between a buyer and a seller where, "you buy from me, I'll buy from you" denotes the basis of the agreement.

5. The cost of goods sold divided by the average dollar value of the inventory kept in stock throughout the year is known as _____ . To calculate the average inventory figure, you add the year's _____ inventory and _____ inventory and then divide by two.

6. Purchasing the appropriate quality, purchasing at the right price and purchasing in the right amount are examples of _____ .

7. A _____ is a list of duties expected of a person in a specific job. A _____ is a list of qualities sought in a job candidate.

8. The practice of allowing employees to make purchases for private use at the company's wholesale price is known as _____. This becomes part of the job description for a buyer who works for a company that gives its employees this benefit.

9. Give three examples of "captive audience" operations that might utilize a materials budget: _____, _____, _____. In these situations, a foodservice provider has usually bid on the contract to provide food for a given amount of time and must estimate expenses to determine what to charge for its services. If the cost of a particular item goes up too much, cutting into profits, the foodservice provider may be forced to seek a substitute for that item.

10. A buyer who spends time learning a housekeeper's daily routine is broadening his or her _____ skills.

Multiple Choice
1. Which of the following is not an example of a possible ethical pitfall for buyers?
   a. free samples
   b. backdoor selling
   c. gifts from suppliers
   d. equipment testing

2. If a company's beginning food inventory is $15,000, its ending inventory is $13,500 and the cost of goods sold is $175,000, what is the inventory turnover?
   a. 18.28
   b. 24.28
   c. 12.28
   d. 14.28

3. The inventory turnover calculated above indicates which of the following?
   a. it takes almost two months for food to leave the receiving dock and end up on a plate
   b. inventory is moving quickly through the operation
   c. inventory is moving very slowly through the operation
   d. it takes approximately two weeks for food to leave the receiving dock and end up on a plate

4. If a buyer were trying to lower his or her AP prices which of the following would he do?
   a. encourage backdoor selling
   b. seek volume discounts
   c. focus exclusively on the EP price
   d. stay with one supplier

5. Which of the following is not a good reason for changing suppliers?
   a. frequent back orders
   b. late deliveries
   c. frequent discount offers
   d. numerous items that must be returned

6. Which of the following would be categorized as an interpersonal skill?
   a. ability to prepare a Fuzzy Navel at the bar
   b. ability to see the organization as a whole
   c. ability to interact with department heads
   d. answers "a" and "b"

7. A buyer might find which of the following to be a roadblock to taking a cash discount?
   a. lack of storage space for the amount of product required to receive the discount
   b. accounting department payment policies
   c. quantity ordering restrictions imposed by the company
   d. none of the above

8. Of the following items, which might be used to evaluate a buyer's performance?
   a. inventory turnover
   b. stockouts
   c. purchases as a percentage of sales volume
   d. all of the above

9. Which of the following might not be a supervisor's expectation of a buyer
   a. to be loyal to the company
   b. to abide by the company's written ethical guidelines
   c. to do whatever it takes to maintain good relationships with colleagues and hourly employees
   d. to avoid legal problems

10. A rough estimate of the appropriate dollar value of inventory is 1% of annual sales. Another estimate is that food inventory should be no more than 1/3 of the average monthly food costs. If a restaurant has $850,000 in food annual food sales and monthly food costs of $36,000, what would be the acceptable inventory values based on these two approximation methods?
    a. $8,500 and $1,200 respectively
    b. $8,500 and $12,000 respectively
    c. $850 and $1,200 respectively
    d. $85,000 and 12,000 respectively

Apply Your Knowledge
1. If you were the buyer for a large independent operation, how would you work out differences with the chef who is blaming you for buying inferior meat cuts, when you really feel like it is inattention to detail in the kitchen that is resulting in higher than usual percentages of waste?

2. You work for a very bottom line-oriented company and have been directed to take every discount that is offered – volume, cash, quantity, etc. How would you explain to your supervisor that it is not always the best idea to meet the requirements for these discounts? Give examples of times when taking the discount could actually result in higher, rather than lower expenditures.

3. Which of the three basic skills of a buyer, technical, human or conceptual, do you think is the most important? Explain.

Chapter 8
The Purchase Specification: An Overall View
After reading this chapter, you should be able to:
- List the information included on purchase specifications.
- Identify factors that influence the information included on purchase specifications.
- Explain the potential problems related to purchase specifications.
- Describe how quality is measured, including the use of government grades and packers' brands.

Outline
1. Introduction
   - Product specification—also called product identification; a description of all the characteristics of a product required to fill a certain production and/or service need
     - Often used by small buyers who shop for products on a day-to-day basis
   - Purchase specification—includes product information, but also related supplier services required by the buyer
     - Often used by large companies that seek long-term relationships with several primary sources
   - Preparing detailed specifications takes time
     - Must learn about product
       - References distributed by the U.S. Department of Agriculture (USDA)
       - Information from product industries
       - Produce Marketing Association (PMA)
2. Why Have Specs?
   - Serve as quality control and cost standards
   - Help to avoid misunderstandings between suppliers, buyers, users and company officials
   - Allow someone to take over when a buyer is absent
   - Serve as useful tools for training assistant buyers and manager trainees
   - Essential when a company wants to obtain bids from other companies
3. Who Decides What to Include on the Specs?
   - Owner manager or other top management official
   - Buyer
   - User
   - Combination of these three
4. What Information Does a Spec Include?
   - Some are formal or lengthy; others are informal or much shorter
   - Government agencies typically prepare formal specifications
   - Hospitality operations sometimes prepare informal specs containing
     - Product yield
     - Quality
     - Packaging
   - Specs may include
     - Performance requirement or intended use of the product
     - Exact name of the product or service
     - Packer's brand name
       - Packers' brands indicate quality
       - Add the word "or equivalent" next to a packer's brand on a spec to allow for flexibility and allow more than one supplier to compete for your business
       - Some buyers use the words "equal to or better" on a spec
       - Sometimes a specific brand is required, perhaps as an ingredient in a recipe

- U.S. quality grade
  - Federal government has developed grades for some items
  - Some items in the channel of distribution may not be graded
- Size information
  - Exact weight
  - Desired weight range
  - Number of items per case, per pound, etc.
- Acceptable trim or acceptable waste
- Package size
- Type of package
  - Not always standardized
  - Some suppliers may scrimp on packaging
  - Packaging can add considerable cost
  - May require recyclable packaging materials
- Preservation and/or processing method
  - Preservation: refrigerated, frozen, canned
  - Processing: smoked, salted, oil-cured, etc.
- Point of origin
  - Exact part of the world
  - Impacts flavor and texture
  - Menu might indicate an item from a certain region
- Packaging procedure
  - Slab-packed—tossed into the container
  - Individually wrapped (more expensive)
  - Number of containers to a case
  - Will the supplier bust a case?
- Degree of ripeness
- Form
  - Cheese in a brick, grated or sliced
  - Beef raw or precooked
- Color
- Trade association standards
- Approved substitutes
- Expiration dates
- Chemical standards
  - Organic vegetables
  - Chemical-free meats
- Test or inspection procedures
- Cost and quantity limitations
  - How much of an item to be purchased at a time
  - Request that the supplier look for a substitute item when cost limits are approached
- General instructions
  - Delivery procedures
  - Credit terms
  - Allowable number of returns and stockouts
  - Whether the product should be delivered to all units in the hospitality company
  - Other supplier services desired like help in devising new uses for a product
- Specifications to bidder
  - Bidding procedures
  - Criteria for supplier selection

- Qualifications and capabilities you expect from supplier

5. What Influences the Types of Information Included on the Spec?
   - Company goals and policies—McDonalds has a Global Antibiotics Policy that requires poultry suppliers not use antibiotics that are in the class of compounds used in human medicine; this needs to be in the specs
   - Time and money available
   - Production systems the hospitality operation uses—if an operation broils rather than grills its burgers, the fat content of the beef needs to be a big higher to compensate for loss of juices if meat is broiled to the well-done state
   - Storage facilities—freezer space may be limited for example
   - Employee skill levels—the lower the level, the more buyers must purchase portion-controlled foods, convenience items and one-step cleaners
   - Menu requirements
   - Sales prices or budgetary limitations
   - Service style—a cafeteria needs menu items that have a long hot-holding life

6. Who Writes the Specs?
   - Company personnel can write the specs
   - Many specs are found in industry publications, CDs, online services and government documents
   - An expert can be hired—USDA inspectors who will also check the products at the supplier's plant to make sure they comply with specs then stamp or seal them to certify compliance
   - Buyer and supplier can work together

7. Potential Problems with Specs
   - If specs contain unreasonable requirements—quality tolerance limits, cost limits, etc.—they will add to AP cost but may not add to value
   - Inadvertent discrimination—indicating that supplier be within 15 miles to ensure quick deliveries, dealing with a supplier 16 miles away could result in legal trouble or eliminate a supplier from the bidding process
   - Spec could request a quality difficult for suppliers to obtain
   - Some specs rely too heavily on government grades
   - Food specifications should not be static—oranges from Florida may not be the best choice on a year-round basis
   - Receiver must be trained to read the specs so he or she doesn't accept merchandise not in accord with the specs
   - Getting hit with the "lowball"
     - "Lowball" is a bid that is low for artificial or dishonest reasons
     - Suppliers may use this tactic to get in the door of a buyer
     - To avoid, buyers should shop around frequently and keep specs current
   - Inequality among bidders
     - If specs are too loose, too many suppliers can meet the minimum requirements
     - Particular problem in fresh produce trade
   - Specifications that are too tight
     - Tend to eliminate suppliers
     - Large companies may want products available on a national basis, this limits number of suppliers who can accommodate national distribution
   - Advertising your own mistakes
   - Redundant favoritism
   - Too many ordering and delivery schedules
   - And always remember

- The object of bid buying is to obtain the lowest possible AP price but if this doesn't translate into an acceptable edible-portion (EP) cost nothing has been accomplished
  - Writing specs helps clarify what is wanted in an item
8. The Optimal Quality to Include on the Spec
   - "Quality" means some standard of excellence
   - Standard could be high quality, medium quality or low quality
   - Quality is something to be decided on by company officials and then maintained
9. Who Determines Quality?
   - Decision must be based on customer expectations
   - Quality affects customers' perceptions of the operation
   - Quality standards for supplies, services and equipment usually come from the top of the company
10. Measures of Quality
    - Federal-government grades
      - USDA has issued quality grade standards for more than 300 food products
      - Government's role is to check the sanitation or production facilities and the wholesomeness of the food product throughout the distribution channel
      - For an item to be graded, it must be produced under continuous federal-government inspection
      - Sometimes a buyer or even a state will require federal grading; for example several states require fresh eggs to carry a federal quality grade shield
      - Graders work under "limiting" rules where an item that receives a low score on one factor, cannot be granted a high grade designation regardless of the total score
      - Problem: graders place an emphasis on appearance, not looking at taste and other culinary factors
      - Other problems include
        - Wide tolerance between grades
        - Grader discretion
        - Deceiving appearance of products
        - Possible irrelevance of grades to EP cost
        - Graders aren't looking at delivery schedule and packaging as part of the overall value
        - Raw food items are not consistent and quality may fluctuate over the year
        - Lack of uniformity of terms used to indicate the varying grade levels
        - Lack of specific regional designation—California and Florida oranges differ greatly throughout the year
    - AP prices—AP prices and quality go hand in hand
    - Packers' Brands
      - Products are produced under manufacturers' brands as well as private labels of an intermediary such as a broadline distributor
      - Buyers may have brand awareness of an easily recognized brand
      - Distribution is a factor
        - National brand
        - Regional brand
      - Products branded with the name of the hospitality operation are usually co-developed by the manufacturer and the operation
      - Packers' brand labels with U.S. grade terminology
        - Hasn't been inspected by USDA personnel
        - In the opinion of the source meets all requirements of the grade indicated
    - Samples
    - Endorsements

- Trade associations
- Your own specifications
  - Buyer will use a combination of information from all of the above to develop quality measures
11. Is the Quality Available?
- Quality of an item may only be available through one supplier
- Easy, but not desirable, to restrict yourself to one supplier not only by quality standards but because of the AP prices you are willing to accept
12. The Buyer's Major Role—maintain the quality standards someone else has determined
13. The Optimal Supplier Services to Include on the Spec
- Requiring specific services may further restrict number of suppliers who can provide what you want
- Bid buying requires that you be able to put up with a variety of supplier capabilities
- Buyers become attached to the supplier services, because there is often not a lot of variation between one product and another

True/False

T F 1. Independent operators often work with their suppliers to develop specifications in spite of the fact that this is not always the best option.

T F 2. The USDA has issued grade standards for more than 1,000 food products.

T F 3. Even though you represent a small independent operation, you will be considered a supplier's best customer if you always insist on taking busted cases.

T F 4. One of the problems with federal graders is that they tend to focus too much on the appearance of a food and not enough on the taste.

T F 5. The customer has input into the determination of quality standards for many items used by an operation.

T F 6. "Count" and "size" are related terms in that the size of a product, say lemons for example, might be expressed as the count or number that would come in a standard- size case.

T F 7. Federal food inspectors have both limiting and partial limiting rules. The limiting rule states that when a food has received a low score in one area, it can't be given a high grade even if its overall point total is high. A partial limiting rule allows inspectors to choose whether or not to invoke the limiting rule.

T F 8. For a food item to be graded, the inspectors simply come in at the end of the production process and evaluate samples of the product.

T F 9. "Color" and "ripeness" are two of the most important items found in a product specification.

T F 10. In come cases, the cost of the packaging can actually exceed the cost of the product itself.

Fill-in-the-Blank
1. One of the items on a product specification sheet might be the acceptable expiration date of the product. Terms vary for this information and include _____ , _____ , _____ , and _____ dates.

2. To give a supplier a bit of leeway in relation to a particular product, a buyer might include the words _____ or _____, indicating that if the requested packer's brand is not available, an appropriate substitute would be accepted.

3. Sometimes a supplier will intentionally come in with a low bid with the hope of gaining more of the buyer's business in the future. This practice is known as _____. Buyers can avoid this practice on the part of suppliers by keeping their specifications current and frequently obtaining bids for specific items.

4. Knowledge of a particular manufacturer's brand is known as _____. Manufacturers' brands may also be referred to as _____. _____ is when a manufacturer uses U.S. grade terminology on its label, indicating that, although not inspected, the product supposedly meets all U.S. requirements for No. 1 graded products.

5. List five problems associated with using U.S. grades as a measure of quality: _____, _____, _____, _____, _____.

6. The packing procedure is an important consideration in relation to the AP price of a product. If a product has been _____, it indicates that the product has tossed into the container rather than individually wrapped and carefully layered. Although the AP price may be lower for a product packed in this manner, it may cost more in the long run due to product damage.

7. When a buyer is ordering individual steaks, he or she might want to include the following in the product specification: _____ or the acceptable weights of the product; the amount of waste or _____ allowed, and the _____, in this case whether it is raw or cooked. Another consideration would be the _____ or the final weight of the product after it has been prepared and is ready to be served.

8. The _____ is a government organization that charges a fee to assist a buyer with developing meat specifications and overseeing the production and delivery of the products .

9. Name three problems with developing specifications: _____, _____, _____.

10. _____ is possibly the most important item to include on a product specification sheet.

Multiple Choice
1. Which of the following items would not normally be found on a product specification?
   a. country of origin
   b. package size
   c. allowable number of returns and stockouts
   d. U.S. quality grade

2. Company goals and policies, menu items and types of service offered in a given operation influence which of the following?
   a. how the buyer handles suppliers
   b. information included in the product specifications
   c. whether the manager or an hourly employee takes receipt of deliveries
   d. how quickly supplier invoices are paid

3. If a product specification is written such that only one supplier can provide the product, this would be a result of :
   a. the specification being too tight
   b. the specification being too lose
   c. the specification concentrating solely on the AP price
   d. none of the above

4. Slicing a tomato to make sure that it doesn't crumble or turn into tomato juice and is appropriate for its intended use in a bacon, lettuce and tomato sandwich, is an example of which of the following?
   a. chemical standards
   b. cost and quantity limitations
   c. test or inspection procedure
   d. approved substitutes

5. A buyer can find sample specifications in which of the following?
   a. federal publications
   b. product association publications
   c. online services
   d. all of the above

6. In a product specification, a buyer might require that a product have a specific place of origin due to which of the following?
   a. government regulations
   b. USDA requirements
   c. truth-in-menu regulations
   d. chemical standards

7. Which of the following is not a reason for developing product specifications?
   a. they provide a record of past purchases
   b. they are useful when training new buyers or manager trainees
   c. they serve as quality and cost guidelines
   d. they help prevent misunderstandings between buyers and suppliers

8. Purchasing organic produce would be an example of a company's:
   a. chemical standards
   b. inspection procedures
   c. cost and quantity limitations
   d. brand loyalty

9. Which of the following would probably not be involved with deciding what to include in a product specification?
   a. buyer
   b. end user of the product
   c. owner-manager or other top official
   d. customer

10. Which of the following does not influence what is included in a product specification?
   a. time and money available
   b. service style
   , c. number of employees
   d. storage facilities

Apply Your Knowledge
1. Discuss the ethical ramifications of product specifications for a buyer.

2. Discuss the concept of "quality," and how this standard can vary from operation to operation and why.

3. Are you surprised that more food products aren't inspected on a regular basis? Discuss your ideas about the importance of food inspections and make suggestions about how and why you would change the system.

Chapter 9
The Optimal Amount
After reading this chapter, you should be able to:
- Calculate the correct order quantities and order times using the par stock, Levinson, and theoretical methods.
- Explain the benefits and problems of using only the theoretical method.

Outline
1. Introduction
   - Correct order size and correct order amount are important keys to inventory management
2. Optimal Inventory Level
   - Goal is to have inventory that will serve operations without unnecessarily tying up dollars
   - Optimal inventory estimators
     - Percentage of sales: inventory of food, beverage and nonfood supplies to be equal to about 1 percent of annual sales volume
     - Inventory equals approximately one-third of normal month's food costs
     - Food inventory should turn over about three times per week
3. Correct Order Size and Order Time: A Common Approach
   - Par stock approach
     - Procedure
       - Accept suppliers' ordering procedures
       - Decide when it is time to order enough to bring stock level of any item up to par; influenced by amount of storage facilities, cost of the item and shelf life of the products
       - Set par stocks for all food, beverage and nonfood items
       - Determine order amount by subtracting what is on hand from the par stock and add in any safety stock
       - Shop around if necessary and enter this order size at the time supplier designates
       - Periodically review stock levels and adjust as needed
     - This is a trial-and-error process
     - Process works for several reasons
       - Predictability of deliveries
       - Hospitality operators change customer offerings infrequently
     - Major drawback is that buyer may lose broader view of inventory management
4. Correct Order Size and Order Time: Another Approach
   - Called the Levinson approach after Charles Levinson who first addressed these ideas in 1989
   - Procedure
     - Accept suppliers' ordering procedures
     - Determine best time to place orders with suppliers
     - Forecast the amount of merchandise that will be needed during the period of time between regularly scheduled deliveries
       - Forecast the expected number of customers based on past history
       - Forecast the number of customers that will order each specific menu offering
         - Create a popularity index for each menu item by dividing the number sold of this item by the total number of all menu items sold
       - Determine the number of raw pounds of each ingredient needed to satisfy projected sales
         - Portion Factor (PF) = 16 oz. / Amount of ingredient needed for one serving (in ounces)
         - Portion Divider (PD) = PF x ingredient's edible-yield percentage

- Edible yield percentage is computed in one of two ways
  - Accept supplier's estimate of edible yield
  - Conduct your own yield tests
- Compute the order sizes for all items – estimated need for an ingredient divided by the PD for that ingredient
  - Adjust order size for stock on hand, safety stock, etc.
  - Shop around if necessary and enter this order size at the time supplier designates
  - Periodically revise order as well as the PD of each ingredient based on different yield percentages of substituted products

5. Correct Order Size and Order Time: Variations of the Levinson Approach
   - Levinson approach good for items purchased in pound units
   - Levinson method can be adapted by changing the PF formula to reflect the unit of purchase
6. Correct Order Size and Order Time: Combination Approach
7. Correct Order Size: A Theoretical Approach
   - Order size influenced by two costs
     - Storage or carrying costs
       - Largest portion is "capital" or "opportunity" cost
       - Storage costs aren't exact, but estimates run from 10 to 25 percent of inventory value
     - Ordering costs
       - Include cost of paperwork, employee wages, etc.
       - Ordering costs aren't exact, estimates range from $20 to $130 per order
     - As storage costs go up (large orders) ordering costs go down (not ordering as often) and vice versa
   - There is an optimal size where ordering costs and storage costs are both as low as possible
   - Economic order quantity (EOQ) formula (see textbook for details)
   - It may be inconvenient or impractical to order EOQ, this figure gives buyers a basis for evaluating other order sizes, and helps them learn to think in terms of ordering and storage costs
8. Correct Order Time: a Theoretical Approach
   - Buyers want to order at some level of inventory greater than zero known as safety stock or reorder point (ROP)
   - Buyers will want to establish a usage pattern over six months or so to determine how many units are used on an average day
   - Lead time is the lag between the time the order is placed and the time it arrives
   - An order should be placed when there is just enough stock to cover use during the lead time
   - After a delivery, a buyer will want to be as close to the EOQ as possible, timing it so that the new order arrives close to the time that the existing product is used up; this is called just-in-time (JIT) inventory
   - JIT inventory is risky
     - Stockout costs are expenses associated with being unable to serve a product because it was not ordered in time
     - Deliveries are pretty predictable, but what if the supplier is out of the needed product
   - Accurate historical records of lead times, usage patterns, safety stocks and supplier capabilities and dependability will determine the success of a buyer's determined ROP
9. Correct Order Size and Order Time: Other Problems with Theoretical Approaches
   - Usage rates vary from day to day
   - Storage and ordering costs vary
   - Stockout costs are difficult to assess
   - A buyer may only quality for once-a-week delivery, not best for EOQ and ROP concepts
   - Difficult to make the decision as to which items to consider for EOQ and ROP

- A supplier buys from someone else – a buyer's EOQ may not be consistent with the supplier's EOQ
- Items get discontinued
- EOQ assumes adequate storage facilities
- EOQ assumes products will be used before spoiling

10. Correct Order Size and Order Time: Benefits of the Theoretical Approach
   - Substitutes fact for fiction
   - There exists a range of order sizes where the total cost per year (ordering and storage costs) doesn't vary dramatically
   - Computers help with calculating EOQ and ROP
   - Large operations can benefit greatly from implementing these concepts

True/False

T F 1. Safety stock is the amount over and above par stock that is maintained or ordered for emergencies or special circumstances such as banquets that are scheduled for the coming week.

T F 2. Stockout costs are easily determined and can be assigned a specific dollar value.

T F 3. A restaurant's "popularity index" helps chefs predict the number of people that will be visiting the restaurant on any given day.

T F 4. The discipline of developing EOQs and ROPs may be as important as obtaining the resulting order quantities and times because it forces a buyer to pay attention to the variables and gives a broader view of the entire inventory process.

T F 5. "Carrying costs" refers to the extra amount charged for emergency delivery services.

T F 6. A buyer who uses only the par stock method for maintaining inventory may not be aware of the storage and other costs for making a large order just to receive a quantity discount. In fact, the storage costs may exceed the discount received.

T F 7. Ordering costs are industry specific and range between $25 and $30 per order for the hospitality industry.

T F 8. A portion factor (PF) of 2 for filet mignon means that each steak serving is 8 ounces.

T F 9. The usage pattern shows how a particular product is used. For example a usage pattern might indicate that 20 dozen egg are used per day on weekends and 15 dozen eggs are used per day on weekdays.

T F 10. A buyer might use the par stock method for maintaining inventory on a regular basis and use the Levinson approach to prepare an order for stock needed for a traditionally busy weekend.

Fill-in-the-Blank

1. _____ is the number of days between the placement of an order and the delivery of the products. This is an important calculation for those who utilize a _____ inventory system or one where the new items arrive on the loading dock just as the last bit of the original stock is supposedly being used in the kitchen.

2. The basic formula for the portion factor (PF) of an item measured by weight is _____.

3. The basic formula for the portion divider (PD) is _____.

4. The _____ or _____ (acronym) is a predetermined level of inventory for a given product, that indicates it is time to place an order for that product.

5. _____ is the term for the money tied up in inventory. This is also known as _____ because if one's money is already invested in one thing it can't be invested in something else.

6. The _____ or the _____ (acronym) is the quantity to order that incurs the least ordering and storage costs throughout the year.

7. To compute the order size using the Levinson approach, you would divide _____ by _____.

8. _____ is a multi-step process for determining the amount of merchandise that will be needed during a specific time period.

9. The actual cost of products used or sold divided by the average inventory value kept at the hospitality operation is known as the _____.

10. The often indeterminate costs of being out of an item requested by a guest is know as _____.

Multiple Choice

1. Deciding when to place an order to bring a product up to par stock involves a number of factors including which of the following:
   a. the supplier's delivery schedule
   b. the cost of the item
   c. the amount of storage available
   d. all of the above

2. Which of the following is not a reason that a par stock ordering system works so well in the hospitality industry?
   a. doesn't take up too much of the buyer's time over the course of a year
   b. delivery schedules are regular
   c. offerings don't change too often—menus and bar offerings stay the same
   d. inventories only a few hundred dollars over "optimum" are usually no concern

3. Your restaurant is known for its "Pound of Potatoes" skillet breakfasts. From experience, you know that the edible yield percentage is 85%, slightly higher than for some potato recipes because you serve the potatoes with the skins. On an average morning, you serve 200 Pound of Potatoes breakfasts, some with sausage and peppers, others with mushrooms and cheese and the most famous, "create your own." Calculate how many AP pounds of potatoes you need to serve 200 persons.
   a. 259 pounds
   b. 230 pounds
   c. 254 pounds
   d. 235 pounds

4. Which of the following inventory approaches requires the buyer to develop a "popularity index" for each menu item?
    a. inventory amount as a percentage of annual sales volume
    b. food-inventory amount as a percentage of monthly food costs
    c. Levinson method
    d. none of the above

5. What is the difference between Chef Hertzman's formula for determining how much to order and Levinson's formula?
    a. the Hertzman formula always comes out higher
    b. the Hertzman formula leaves out the step for calculating the portion factor
    c. the Hertzman formula doesn't take into account the number of servings
    d. none of the above

6. Trying to maintain a just-in-time inventory system indicates that you:
    a. trust the delivery services of your suppliers
    b. see no need to do the theoretical calculations of other inventory systems
    c. will tolerate a more than average amount of spoilage
    d. like to have a cushion of safety stock, just in case

7. Which of the following will help ensure the success of an inventory management system based on the economic order quantity (EOQ)?
    a. supplier back orders
    b. discontinuation of a product
    c. inadequate storage facilities
    d. enough historical data to create a fairly accurate usage pattern of a product

8. Which of the following is not a step in the Levinson approach to inventory management.
    a. obtain a year's worth of cost data about the specific product
    b. accept delivery schedule
    c. determine best time to place orders
    d. forecast amount of needed merchandise

9. Using the par stock approach, you would subtract what is on hand from the par stock and then do what before placing the order?
    a. add the safety stock
    b. subtract the safety stock
    c. ignore the safety stock
    d. none of the above

10. Food inventories should turnover approximately how many times?
    a. 3 times per month
    b. 2 times per month
    c. 3 times per week
    d. 2 times per week

Apply Your Knowledge
1. Discuss how a company might balance a par stock system with a theoretical inventory system and why it might want to consider such a plan.

2. All of the inventory management systems—par stock concept, Levinson theory or theoretical— require historical data. Imagine that you are a new buyer in a hotel/restaurant operation, discuss how you would assemble the information you would need to use each of the inventory management systems and how you would obtain that information.

3. Explain how a "theoretical approach" can substitute "fiction" for "fact."

Chapter 10
The Optimal Price
After reading this chapter, you should be able to:
- Explain how purchase prices influence buyers.
- Describe how suppliers determine their purchase prices.
- Identify methods buyers employ to reduce purchase prices.
- Calculate cost information, including edible portion cost, servable portion cost, and standard cost.
- Evaluate the advantage of an opportunity buy.

Outline
1. Introduction
   - Optimal price: the price that when combined with optimal quality and supplier services produces the optimal value
   - Optimal price is the lowest possible edible-portion (EP) cost while maintaining the optimal value
   - Lowest EP cost may or may not be lowest as-purchased (AP) price
   - Buyers must be able to translate AP price into the EP price: EP cost = AP price/edible yield percentage
2. How AP Prices Influence Buyers
   - Two extremes
     - Buyers that focus on AP prices alone
     - Buyers that focus on quality and supplier services
     - Most buyers fall somewhere in the middle, leaning toward one extreme or the other depending on the product itself
   - Suppliers want to know their buyers' reactions to AP prices
     - Novice buyers overrate AP prices
     - Price usually follows quality
       - There is a point where price continues to rise and quality fails to rise
       - Hard to assess with new products
     - Derived demand – the hospitality customers' demands for the product
       - Price conscious hospitality customers signal a supplier that the buyer will also be price conscious
       - Price may be secondary; suppliers will realize this when ultimate consumers are not price conscious
     - Price may be secondary if supplier is exclusive carrier of one or more items
     - Buyer who seeks an itemized bill is price conscious
     - If the products represent a huge expense, buyer will be more price conscious
     - Buyers on a tight budget tend to get more price conscious as the budget period ends
       - Hard times force buyers to examine AP prices more thoroughly
       - Many buyers will look at adding their own economic values; example: purchasing raw food ingredients instead of a prepared menu item
3. How AP Prices are Determined
   - AP prices as a function of the suppliers costs
     - Suppliers add all operating and nonoperating costs and try to allocate a portion to each service and product they sell plus predetermined profit markups
     - Some products have "rules"; example: fresh tomato market might have a rule of three whereby a supplier will re-sell the tomatoes for three times the cost
     - If suppliers think their markup will make the AP price too high to be accepted by buyers they have several options
       - Lower the AP cost
       - Add supplier services to justify the cost

- Refuse to carry the item
- Average supplier earns after-tax profit of only about 1 to 3 percent
- AP prices as a function of supply and demand
  - Supply and demand has largest impact at beginning of the distribution channel
  - Most suppliers want to reduce the supply and demand effect
    - Risky to carry items other suppliers can duplicate
    - Suppliers differentiate themselves with services
- AP prices as a function of competitive pressure
  - Differentiation of services is key
- Buyer pricing
  - Suppliers like this best of all
  - Often occurs when a supplier assists in developing specs
  - Happens when a buyer consistently runs out of items and engages in "panic buying"

4. Ways to Reduce AP Price so that Overall Value is Increased
   - Best to pay less for a product while maintaining quality and services
   - Superiors immediately appreciate a reduced AP cost
   - Buyers need to ensure that purchased item continues to fulfill intended use
   - Buyer should consider the time it takes to negotiate new prices
   - Make-or-buy analysis
     - Should be performed periodically
     - Buyer must be careful to not underestimate or not include all costs
   - Provide your own supplier services and/or economic values
     - Example: buy from a no-frills wholesale club
     - Example: "forklift discount" where buyers unload their own deliveries
   - Shop around more frequently
     - Line-item purchasing: obtaining competitive bids for several products from two or more suppliers and "cherry picking" the supplier who is lowest for each item
     - Suppliers prefer bottom-line, firm-price purchasing where buyer purchases from the supplier with the lowest total price for the group of items
   - Lower the quality standard
   - Blanket orders
     - Form of volume discount
     - Usually includes a large order for several low-cost items
     - Even though AP costs may not be lower, you reduce annual ordering costs
   - Improved negotiations
   - Substitutions
     - When AP prices get too high, buyers can do the following:
       - Pay the price and pass it on to consumer
       - Lower the quality and/or reduce supplier services and economic values provided to the hospitality operation's customers
       - Drop the item
       - Carry a substitute
   - Cash discounts
     - Suppliers may accept a lower AP price provided they receive cash in advance, at the time of delivery or shortly thereafter
     - Buyer must consult accounting department and management to make sure such an arrangement is possible
     - Extremely economical way to lower AP price, however may tie up funds needed for other things

- o Cash rebate: pay full price up front but after showing proof-of-purchase will receive cash back; must take into consideration cost of reproducing bills, etc.
- Hedging
  - o Process of maintaining a certain AP price in a fluctuating market (dairy products for example) by purchasing futures contracts
  - o Several problems arise
    - A lot of cash could be tied up (minimum amount of product is large)
    - Hedging can be done for only a few items
    - Transaction costs are involved
    - Time intensive activity
    - Transaction costs might overpower benefits
    - Possible that no one would purchase contract when the time came to sell it (although unlikely)
- Economical packaging
  - o More standard packaging should reduce the AP price
  - o Efficient packaging reduces storage needs
  - o Large volume packs are usually cheaper per unit of weight than smaller counterparts
- Odd-hour deliveries
  - o Early morning or night deliveries
  - o Sacred hour deliveries between 11:30 A.M. to 1: 30 P.M.
- Co-op purchasing
  - o Definition: group of buyers from different hospitality organizations who pool individual small orders to receive volume discounts
- Cost-plus purchasing
  - o Definition: buyer purchases goods at supplier's cost (known as the landed cost) plus an agreed-upon profit markup
  - o Buyer must be willing to accept risk of costs to supplier going up
  - o If profit markup is a percentage, suppliers may not work to control costs
  - o Supplier must be willing to show proof of costs if asked
  - o Buyers may need to follow this strategy if they want long-term contractual arrangements with their suppliers
- Promotional discounts
  - o Definition: rebate from the supplier that the buyer's company must use to promote the retail sale of the product
  - o Example: 2 percent rebate on cheesecake if you agree to promote the product in your restaurant
- Exchange bartering
  - o Exchanging one's products for another's
  - o Might have to join a barter group that has a membership fee
  - o Direct bartering: where one deals directly with another business
  - o May have image problem or price gouging or limited selection
  - o IRS is looking at bartering; "trade" dollars must be reported correctly
- Introductory offers
- Reevaluate EP Costs
  - o Buyers should habitually revise the portion divider (PD) and portion factor (PF) for foods
  - o Buyers should also evaluate existing and possible products by dividing the AP price per pound (or liter, etc) by that ingredient's PD and you have the EP cost for one serving of that ingredient
  - o Buyers will find this information helpful, but so will managers and supervisors

- Pre-costing a menu involves calculating each item's standard cost (see textbook for formula)
- Menu prices are calculated by dividing the standard cost by the target product cost percentage
- Standard costs can also be used in the overall cost control system
- Total actual costs for a menu item can be calculated as follows: Beginning inventory (in dollars) of items in the dinner + purchases for the month = inventory available for the month – inventory at the end of the month = actual cost

5. Opportunity Buys
   - Suppliers offer opportunity buys for several reasons
     - Normal quantity discount for large purchases of one item
     - Volume discounts for large purchases of several items
     - Blowout sale, buyout sale or closeout sale: include items that must be sold at a loss for whatever reason
     - Muzz-go lists: items that are on the verge of spoiling or are of poorer quality
     - Suppliers might have received a good buy and want to share the savings
     - Suppliers may be cash-starved
     - New suppliers may be trying to break into a market
     - Suppliers may be introducing a new product
   - Buyers must evaluate both the quantitative and qualitative factors of an opportunity buy
   - Buyers must look at relevant storage costs
   - Buyers might consider the following questions about the opportunity buy:
     - Is the quality the same?
     - What is the probability of a large decrease in the item's AP price after the buy?
     - Are cash reserves available?
     - Are storage facilities available?
     - What is the storage life of the product?
     - Will insurance premiums and other things increase as a result of the buy?
     - Will personal property taxes increase?
     - Will the usage rate of the item remain the same over the next few weeks or months?
     - Does this buy require a change of suppliers?
     - Are the supplier services the same?
     - Is the opportunity legitimate?
     - Is the buy "legal?"
     - Is the supplier licensed?
     - Do the items actually belong to creditors?
     - Are the items in good shape (e.g., not thawed after having been frozen)?
     - Is the item for sale "as-is, where-is?"

True/False

T F 1. A truly experienced buyer will concentrate on the AP price to the exclusion of all other quality factors.

T F 2. The closer a product is to its original source, the more variable the price will be for that product.

T F 3. The AP price is not a stand-alone factor, it must be considered with the EP cost, product quality and supplier services.

T F 4.   Buyer fact sheets are kept in the purchasing office and pertain to the purchasing history of high-end products.

T F 5.   When AP prices are developed as a function of supply and demand, it indicates that there is little difference between the products of supplier "A" and supplier "B." Suppliers usually do not like the supply and demand effect.

T F 6.   Suppliers appreciate buyers who cherry pick the lowest items form a multi-item bid because they know that all bidders may receive an order or two.

T F 7.   Buyers should continuously be looking for ways to lower AP prices including conducting make-or-buy analyses, considering taking on supplier services and shopping around and investigating new suppliers.

T F 8.   Substitution may be a viable alternative when AP prices for a product get too high.

T F 9.   Buyers normally come out on top when they participate in the pricing process unless they are in a panic buying situation requiring emergency deliveries.

T F 10. Changing your packaging requirements may not only save you money, it may save in storage costs as different container shapes stack better and take up less room than others.

Fill-in-the-Blank
1.   A _____ is an order of miscellaneous items that is often of such a volume that a discount is offered. Additional savings may be experienced with this type of order in that it can save on ordering costs and usually results in only minimal storage costs.

2.   When a buyer accepts a supplier's cost for a product plus either a percentage or a fixed price it is known as _____. Even though this often locks a supplier into a long-term contract, he or she is usually comfortable with this arrangement, knowing that they will always have a certain dollar amount of profit on each item. The supplier's cost is sometimes referred to as the _____.

3.   The buyer, in the purchasing procedure above must be willing to accept some element of risk and should have the right to review the supplier's records to confirm that the correct AP price has been charged. In addition, the buyer must make sure that the supplier doesn't subcontract products to their friends, creating a _____ type of distribution channel.

4.   _____ is when a buyer seeks bids on a number of products and agrees to buy all of the included products from the lowest bidder.

5.   Similar to a cash discount is the _____ where the supplier will send cash back after receiving a proof of purchase. Buyers should take into account the personnel costs of such an offer as it requires making copies, mailing the proof and ensuring that the check is actually received.

6.   _____ is the practice of buying futures for a product, such as butter, to help ensure that the actual expenditures are as close as possible to the budgeted amount.

7.   _____ is where one trades product or services for needed products or services.

8. The process by which a buyer determines whether to cut down on the purchase of prepared foods and prepare those items onsite is called the _____.

9. Replacing one item with another because of lack of availability or too high of an AP price is known as _____.

10. There are usually no guarantees of quality on items purchased at an auction, nor are there usually any supplier services such as deliveries. A buyer must be willing to accept the item in an _____ condition.

Multiple Choice

1. Which of the following might tip off your supplier's salesperson that the AP price is of significant interest to you?
   a. your operation has a reputation known for its "good prices"
   b. you have not been known to shop around for new suppliers
   c. you are an experienced buyer
   d. you have never asked for an itemized bill

2. When would price not necessarily follow quality?
   a. if the item is hard to find
   b. if the item requires a special delivery vehicle
   c. if the item is in high demand
   d. all of the above

3. There are many ways a buyer can lower the AP price of a product. Which of the following would not lower a product's AP price?
   a. buying enough to qualify for a volume discount
   b. ordering a custom product
   c. taking advantage of opportunity buys
   d. opting for economical packaging

4. Which of the following is not true of the pricing procedure where AP prices are set as a function of the supplier's cost?
   a. the AP price is the cost of the item, plus a percentage profit markup and a portion of the operating and non-operating costs of doing business
   b. some suppliers may use an industry-wide rule of thumb for pricing an item
   c. buyers often have input into the pricing process
   d. a supplier will often refuse to carry an item if the profit margin is too low

5. A quick way to reduce the AP price while increasing value is to pay less for the product while maintaining quality and equal supplier services. Which of the factors below should be considered when pursuing such an option?
   a. the product must meet the demands of the intended use
   b. the buyer should keep in mind the time it takes to research product options or negotiate a lower price
   c. a poor substitute may save money but may alienate users and customers
   d. all of the above

6.	Your run a restaurant at a truckstop where you serve meals 24-hours a day and operate with employees who are semi-skilled at best. Which of the following discounts might be of particular interest?
	a. a volume closeout sale
	b. odd-hour deliveries
	c. cash discounts
	d. none of the above

7.	When you are determining the portion factor you divide the number of ounces in a pound by what number?
	a. the number of ounces in a serving size
	b. the number of portions you are serving
	c. the number of portions you hope to get out of a pound
	d. the portion divider

8.	A buyer might consider hedging for which of the following reasons?
	a. to make a profit and offset the cost of another product
	b. to avoid impact of market price fluctuations on the budget
	c. to make an impression on his or her boss
	d. to drive down the price of the product futures

9.	Suppliers like it best when AP prices are:
	a. based on supplier's cost
	b. based on supply and demand
	c. developed by the panicked buyer
	d. based on competitive pressure

10.	Which of the following is usually not the main problem with opportunity buys?
	a. the available items may be owned by creditors
	b. the items may be for sale by unlicensed dealers
	c. the damage to the items may not be visible
	d. you may already have par stock for the items available

Apply Your Knowledge

1.	Cash discounts can be attractive money-savers, so much so, that some companies have even borrowed money to take advantage of these offers. Discuss all of the costs associated with borrowing money and whether you think those costs can be justified.

2.	Maintaining a database of edible portion costs for the majority of products used in an operation can benefit the company beyond the confines of the purchasing department. Discuss how this information could benefit managers, chefs and others in the organization.

3.	As a buyer, you are considering several methods to reduce the AP prices and improve the bottom line. Your supplier has given you several options including a "fork-lift discount" and a fairly impressive discount for accepting deliveries during the sacred hours of 11:30 am to 1:30 pm two days a week and after 11 pm on Saturdays. List the number of people you would need to talk to before engaging in such an arrangement and the additional costs that might be incurred.

Chapter 11
The Optimal Payment Policy

After reading this chapter, you should be able to:
- Identify the major objective of a payment policy.
- Explain the costs of paying sooner than necessary and of paying too late.
- Compare the bill-paying procedures that can be employed by hospitality operators.

Outline
1. Introduction
   - Buyers have little influence on payment policies
   - Buyers should be involved however
     - Payment terms, discounts, etc., are supplier services and the buyer uses them in value analyses
     - Buyer needs to know which supplier services to negotiate for
     - Quick payment requirements of opportunity buys
     - Stalled suppliers are not eager to negotiate with buyers
2. The Objective of Payment Policy
   - Keep money as long as possible
   - Pay bills at correct time
   - Collect monies due as quickly as possible
3. Cost of Paying Sooner than Necessary
   - Theoretical cost based on lost opportunities
     - Interest in savings account or CD
     - Ability to make other purchases
     - Ability to take advantage of opportunity buys
     - Ability to take care of emergencies
4. Cost of Paying Too Late
   - Gain reputation as a slow payer
   - Jeopardize future credit potential
   - Damage credit ratings
   - Be put on a cash-on-delivery (COD) basis
   - Incur interest and/or penalty charges
   - Lose cash discounts or other AP lowering opportunities
   - Incur legal difficulties
   - Lose suppliers
   - Be limited to working with suppliers with few services and low-grade products
5. What is the Best Policy?
   - Best policy is one that allows one to keep money as long as possible unless there are incentives to do otherwise (e.g., cash discounts)
   - Average hospitality operation is not in a position to negotiate payment terms, most on COD basis
   - Often interest is charged on unpaid balances
   - Large operations are able to negotiate and often have a 45-day window for making payments
   - Small operators should set aside a specific time each week to pay bills, eliminating need to juggle bills and payment periods throughout the year
6. The Mechanics of Bill Paying
   - Paid-outs – cash is removed from the register to pay driver upon delivery
   - Invoices on account – invoices are tallied and a statement is sent at the end of the month
   - Credit card payments – Buyer uses credit card to pay for purchases at the end of the credit period

- Bill-paying service – buyer pays outside service to pay bills and ensure purchases meet buyer's expectations (usually in a construction setting)
7. Another Word About Discounts
    - Large operations usually have more opportunities to take advantage of discounts
    - There are problems with discounts
        - Company may focus on discounts and lose sight of real cost of the purchase
        - Cash discounts may interfere with normal accounts payable schedule
        - Company may stay with a discounting supplier longer than it should (if providing inferior foods or slacking on services)
        - Borrowing money to take advantage of discounts may be costly
        - If items need to be returned, the company needs to know if cash discount periods are extended

True/False

T F 1.   The percentage of sales fees that a supplier will be charged when a buyer pays with a credit card may be offset by the fact that the money is available within 2 to 3 days and is available to be reinvested in inventory. The administrative services provided by the credit card company may result in additional savings.

T F 2.   Stretching the accounts payable is a good practice in the hospitality industry.

T F 3.   The opportunity costs of taking a cash discount probably need to be examined more closely in a large operation than in a small one.

T F 4.   A buyer who focuses on lowering the AP cost of products will always want to take the cash discount if possible.

T F 5.   Establishing the optimal payment policy is a balancing act between paying too early and losing the use of that money and paying too late and possibly damaging the company's relationships with its suppliers.

Fill-in-the-Blank

1.   A _____ supplier is one who hasn't been paid within the credit period and is probably getting concerned about when a payment will be made.

2.   A company who is known to be a slow payer or in financial difficulties is known as a bad _____ and will often be put on a _____ or _____ (acronym) basis where it must pay for the purchase when the delivery is made.

3.   An _____ account is one where money is deposited for use by a third party to pay the bills associated with a specific project.

4.   Keeping your money as long as possible, paying your bills at the correct time and collecting monies due as fast as possible are all goals of _____.

5.   The _____ is the amount of time a supplier will give a company to pay its bills without charging interest or late fees.

Multiple Choice

1. Your supplier always offers you a 2% cash discount if you pay by cash or check within 10 days of receiving your delivery. If you are interested in lowering your AP price, which route will you take?
   a. pay the amount owed within ten days
   b. pay the amount owed within thirty days
   c. either one, the savings in both cases are equal
   d. do none of the above

2. In the question above, what other costs should be considered when making the decision?
   a. carrying costs
   b. ordering costs
   c. opportunity costs
   d. none of the above

3. To a buyer, what might be a disadvantage of using a credit card to pay for supplies?
   a. annual credit card fee
   b. interest charged on unpaid balances
   c. fee for late payments
   d. all of the above

4. Which of the following might you not expect to find on an end-of-period statement?
   a. supplier's operating costs apportioned out to each item
   b. itemized product charges
   c. applicable discounts
   d. interest charges if applicable

5. What is the typical credit period for the hospitality industry?
   a. 60 to 90 days
   b. 30 to 45 days
   c. 20 to 45 days
   d. 45 to 60 days

Apply Your Knowledge

1. Describe how a company might use all four bill-paying procedures at different times for different types of purchases.

2. Why might a supplier not offer a "cash discount" on an invoice paid with a credit card even though he or she will receive the money within the discount period.

Chapter 12
The Optimal Supplier
After reading this chapter, you should be able to:
- Determine a buying plan by selecting a single supplier or bid buying.
- Explain additional criteria used when choosing suppliers.
- Describe the relationship between suppliers and buyers.
- Describe the relationship between salespersons and buyers.

Outline
1. Introduction
   - Buyers usually choose suppliers
   - Owner-manager may choose suppliers
     - Reciprocal buying arrangement
     - Approved supplier-list
2. The Initial Survey
   - Compile list of all suppliers
     - Phone directories
     - Trade directories
     - Trade magazines
     - Other hospitality operators
     - National buying guides and directories
     - Trade shows and conventions
   - Large operators have lengthy list of suppliers; small operators have a more limited number
   - Three problems in conducting initial survey
     - Determining who should be on the list
     - Indiscriminate culling can eliminate a good potential supplier
     - Search can be time-consuming when buyer is seeking a unique item
3. Trimming the Initial List
   - Examining the following
     - Product quality
     - AP price
     - Supplier services
       - Evaluation is often a matter of taste
       - Prompt deliveries
       - Rejected deliveries
       - How adjustments handled on rejected deliveries
       - How well supplier performs on one or two trial deliveries
       - Capacity of the plant
       - Technological know-how
4. The Relationship of Purchasing Policy to Supplier Selection
   - Example: does your company want to work with one supplier and establish long-term contracts for some items
5. Buying Plans
   - Two basic plans
     - Least used: buyer selects a supplier and they work together to meet buyer's needs
       - Used when a reciprocal buying plan exists
       - Used when only one supplier provides item needed
       - Used when buyer or owner-manager trusts supplier's ability, integrity or judgment

- Buyer wants to establish a long-term relationship with a supplier (usually in small operations, a practice called one-stop shopping)
  - Used most often: buyer prepares lengthy specifications for items needed and uses bid-buying procedures
    - Obtaining the lowest bid does not guarantee lowest edible-portion cost
    - Fixed bid
      - Used for large quantities of products purchased over time
      - Formal process with a request for bid or request for quote on specific products or services
      - Bidders usually reply with sealed bids
      - Buyer opens bids and awards business to supplier with lowest bid or bid that that has the highest value per dollar
    - Daily bid (also known as daily quotation buying, call sheet buying, open-market buying, market quote buying)
      - Often used for fresh items or small order of items
      - Informal process
      - Suppliers are given copies of specifications
      - When it is time to order, buyer calls suppliers and asks for bids
      - Buyer records bids or analyzes them electronically
      - Buyer usually chooses supplier with lowest AP price
    - Some suppliers may balk at bid buying
      - AP prices may appear high because of extra supplier services
      - Feel that other bidders are not in their league
      - Competing bidders may inflate prices even though they do not offer services to warrant those prices
6. Other Supplier Selection Criteria
   - Cost-plus purchasing
   - One-stop shopping (also known as sole-source procurement, prime-vendor procurement, single-source procurement)
     - Advantages
       - Reduces ordering costs
       - Buyer may qualify for volume discounts
     - Disadvantages
       - Reduction in supplier selection flexibility
       - Buyer may spend more for products than if he or she had shopped around
   - Stockless purchasing
     - Forward buying: when a buyer purchases a large amount of product (for example a three-month supply) and takes delivery of the entire shipment
     - Stockless purchasing: when a buyer purchases a large amount of product but the supplier stores it for him or her
       - Used when items may become unavailable or AP price may go up
       - Used when purchasing items with company logo
   - Cash and carry (also known as will-call purchasing)
   - Standing orders
     - A supplier's delivery person brings stock up to par stock level
     - Often used for milk or bread
   - Use of technology
     - For some buyers, it may be important that a supplier offer some form of e-procurement option

- Co-op purchasing
  - Advantage: low AP price for those who consolidate buying power
  - Disadvantage: time it takes to manage organization; also may limit a buyer's input on supplier selection
  - Experiencing a renewed popularity due to buying services that have emerged to streamline the process
- Local merchant-wholesaler or national source?
  - Small operators usually deal with local suppliers
  - Large operators sometimes go directly to the source for a product
- Delivery schedule
- Ordering procedure required by supplier
- Credit terms
- Minimum order requirement
- Variety of merchandise
- Lead time
- Free samples
- Return policy
- Reciprocal buying
- Willingness to barter
- Cooperation in bid procedures
- Size of firm
- Number of back orders
- Substitution capability
- Buyout policy
- Suppliers' facilities
- Outside (independent) delivery service
  - Buyers should be wary of suppliers who use no-name delivery services that have no verifiable tracking numbers
  - Independent delivery people usually cannot rectify mistakes on the spot or take refused merchandise
- Long-term contracts
- Case price
  - Example: supplier sells individual items at the case price (sells a can of tomatoes for $2 when a case of 6 cans is usually $12)
  - Sometimes suppliers will bust a case, but usually charge a premium
- Bonded suppliers
  - Does supplier have insurance to cover cost of possible damage to buyer's property?
  - Related issue: Is supplier licensed?
- Consulting service provided
  - Product specifications
  - Preparation and handling procedures
  - Nutrition information
  - Merchandising techniques
- Deposits required
- Willingness to sell storage
- Suppliers who own hospitality operations
  - Disadvantage: supplier is also competitor
  - Advantage: supplier understands the business
- Socially responsible suppliers

- Some buyers won't work with a supplier who:
  - Sells products manufactured by people in foreign countries who do not receive a basic level of wages
  - Sells products the manufacturing of which damages the earth
- Some buyers prefer to work with suppliers who are minority-owned, employ minorities or work with minority-owned subcontractors
- References
7. Most Important Supplier Selection Criteria
  - Most buyers interested first, in product quality
  - Supplier services come in second
  - AP prices comes in third for most, but not all suppliers
8. Make a Choice
9. Supplier-Buyer Relations
  - Supply house officers set the tone of their business
    - Establish quality standards
    - Determine supplier services
    - Plan advertising and promotion campaigns
  - Supply house officers set the overall sales strategies
    - Push strategy: salespeople are urged to do whatever it takes to entice the buyer to purchase product
    - Pull strategy: supplier advertises items to the general public who in turn request these items at the restaurant and thus "pull" the product through the channel
    - Most suppliers use a mix of these two strategies
  - Supply house officers sponsor a great deal of product and market research
    - Items on buyer fact sheets or buyer profiles
      - Buyer's impression of supplier's reputation
      - Major characteristics of buyer's customers
      - Buyer's concern with AP prices
      - Buyer's concern with fast, dependable deliveries
      - Buyer's willingness to experiment with new products
      - Buyer's confidence in his or her purchasing skills
      - Buyer's other duties
      - Buyer's willingness to accept substitutions
      - Buyer's willingness to enter into a reciprocal buying arrangement
      - Company's payment history
      - Buyer's treatment of suppliers and sales persons
      - Buyer's temperament (e.g., easily annoyed, easy to get along with, etc.)
  - Suppliers train their sales staffs
  - Suppliers keep their sales persons' promises
8. Salesperson-Buyer Relationships
  - Buyers must set ground rules with salesperson or distributor sales representative (DSR)
  - Possible sales tactics
    - Backdoor selling
    - Use of free samples to interest/obligate buyer
    - Seeking justifications for their presence
    - Trying to steal buyers from current suppliers
    - Trying to be invited to return
  - Dealing with DSRs is time-consuming, but must be done
  - Buyers can find information on sales tactics and strategies so they know what to look for

9. Evaluating Suppliers and Salespersons
    • Buyer should occasionally evaluate supplier/salesperson performance
    • Buyers should look for consistency of quality, supplier services, etc.
10. Getting Comfortable
    • Supplier selection is not something to do once; process should occasionally be revisited
    • However, supplier changes should only be done after thought and consideration

True/False

T F 1. Buyers must focus only on fixing quality standards and economic values.

T F 2. When a company official insists that a buyer purchase from a certain supplier, this usually means that some sort of reciprocal buying arrangement has been reached or that the owner-manager has prepared an approved-supplier list without consulting the buyer.

T F 3. Large corporations do not need to take the time to compile lengthy lists of suppliers because whatever supplier they choose will give them the best prices available to do business with them.

T F 4. Most small operators prefer to use a limited number of suppliers who carry most of the required items.

T F 5. Operators may contact only one supplier for such items as liquor and dairy products because the middlemen dealing in these product lines usually have few competitors.

T F 6. Buyers can easily narrow their initial list into an approved supplier list by looking only at each supplier's product quality, as-purchased (AP) price, and supplier services.

T F 7. Large corporations have a bit more latitude than small operators in formulating their preferred buying policies and then convincing suppliers to cooperate.

T F 8. Bid buying works well and is simple because suppliers are created equal.

T F 9. Buyers need to remember that obtaining the lowest bid ensures the lowest edible-portion (EP) cost.

T F 10. Usually, buyers use the fixed bid for large quantities of products purchased over a reasonably long period of time.

Fill-in-the-Blank

1. An easy way to narrow a supplier list is by trial and error. However, a supplier's poor performance can leave buyers without a _____ .

2. Deciding whether to use one-stop shopping or bid buying is a matter of _____ for buyers.

3. The _____ bid is often used for fresh items such as fresh produce.

4. Buyers use the formal bidding process, called a _____, for large quantities of products purchased over a reasonably long period of time.

5. When a buyer purchases a large amount of product and takes delivery of the entire shipment, the procedure is referred to as _____.

6. Some buyers are migrating away from one-stop shopping and using _____ as a method to shop around for suppliers.

7. All hospitality operations have preferences regarding the day and time when they accept deliveries from their suppliers. Most would prefer a _____ delivery.

8. Cash discounts, quantity discounts, volume discounts, cash rebates and promotional discounts; when payments are due (i.e., the credit period); the billing procedures; the amount of interest charges buyers may have to pay on the outstanding balance; and the overall installment payment options available are known as _____.

9. The best relationship is one in which both the buyer and the seller are _____.

10. As buyers complete their basic buying plan, _____ and _____ guide them toward the optimal suppliers. Buyers do not want too many restrictions placed on their basic buying plan.

Multiple Choice
1. Local suppliers' names can be gathered from:
    a. local telephone directories
    b. local trade directories
    c. other hospitality operators
    d. all of the above

2. When evaluating the performance of supplier services, buyers should be interested in all of the following except:
    a. prompt deliveries
    b. number of rejected deliveries and how adjustments are handled
    c. how well they take care of one or two trial orders
    d. free samples

3. The fixed-bid buying plan usually begins with the buyer:
    a. sending a "request for bid" to prospective suppliers
    b. sending a sealed bid to the top three suppliers
    c. requesting a financial statement from the supplier
    d. requesting a quote for deliverable goods

4. Cost-plus purchasing is defined as:
    a. purchasing as many items as possible from one supplier
    b. purchasing a large amount of product and taking delivery of the entire shipment
    c. purchasing products for the price suppliers paid, plus an agreed-upon profit markup
    d. banding together several small operators to consolidate their buying power.

5. Credit terms do not include the following:
    a. cash discounts
    b. co-op purchasing
    c. interest rates
    d. billing procedures

6. Supplier salespersons who utilize laptop computers equipped with cellular communication capabilities can:
    a. hasten the order procedure by shortening the lead time
    b. verify product availability
    c. eliminate inaccuracies
    d all of the above

7. All suppliers:
    a. participate in e-marketplaces
    b. offer computer-based communication solutions
    c. want to be competitive
    d. offer delivery services

8. In regards to evaluating a potential supplier's storage and handling abilities, buyers should be concerned about all of the following except the:
    a. delivery facilities
    b. facilities' sanitation
    c. delivery vehicles
    d. the salesperson's sales territory

9. Which of the following supplier selection criteria traits are considered to be important by buyers?
    a. consistency
    b. dependable service
    c. value
    d. all of the above

10. The daily-bid method is also known as all of the following except:
    a. daily quotation buying
    b. short-order buying
    c. call sheet buying
    d. market quote buying

Apply Your Knowledge

1. Compile a list of 15 suppliers using the national buying guides and directory websites identified early in the chapter.

2. Compile a list of trade shows and conventions coming to your area in the next three years by checking the websites included earlier in the chapter.

3. What are the three major time-consuming problems that arise whenever an initial survey is undertaken?

Chapter 13
Typical Ordering Procedures

After reading this chapter, you should be able to:
- Explain the use of a purchase requisition.
- Describe the elements of a purchase order and its use.
- Recognize methods to streamline the ordering process.

Outline

1. Introduction
   - Buying responsibilities end when buyer turns products over to end-user
   - There is a range of formal and informal buying systems
2. Purchase Requisitions
   - Definition: list of needed items or services
   - Usually cover items not ordered on regular basis
   - Disadvantages
     - Too many people involved in deciding types and qualities of products and services
     - Invites backdoor selling
     - Requires time and effort to implement/maintain such a system
   - Advantages
     - Useful training device for department heads who want to become full-time buyers
     - Can relieve a buyer of responsibility for ordering mistakes
     - Can relieve buyer of paperwork
     - Helps provide control of product use in different department
3. Ordering Procedures
   - Buyer determines amount to order
   - Buyer prepares purchase orders (POs)
   - Buyer sends purchase orders to suppliers (keeping copies for records)
   - The actual purchase order form varies from operation to operation, but basic information is the same
   - Buyers may actually place the order in a number of ways:
     - By handing the delivery person the PO
     - By calling or faxing in the order
     - By sending the order via email
     - By sending the order via the internet
   - Management usually decides which ordering procedure to use
4. The Purchase Order
   - Purchase order resembles a purchase requisition
   - Information includes
     - Date
     - Transportation requirement
     - Packaging instructions
     - Quantity
     - Item type
     - Unit size
     - Unit price
     - Extended price
   - Operations use different number of copies of the PO
     - Supplier -- original
     - Second supplier copy – to use as a bill
     - Third supplier copy—for initialing and to send back to the buyer

        o Buyer copy
        o Receiving clerk copy
        o Requisitioner copy
        o Accountant or bookkeeper copy
        o Head office copy
- Most common for three copies to be made
- Company may have LPOs or limited purchase orders which restrict a buyer from purchasing over a certain amount on a single PO
- POs are part of the control chain
  - Minimum control – PO is used to compare with actual deliveries

5. Change Order
6. Expediting
   - Buyer's effort to monitor suppliers from day to day to ensure that products and services arrive at the right time in the right condition
   - Can be used at special times, such as a banquet requiring steaks
   - Often used with FFE that have a habit of showing up late
7. Streamlining the Ordering Procedure
   - Blanket order
   - Purchase order draft system
     - Definition: PO with a check to cover the cost attached
     - Supplier can also charge a buyer's credit or debit card
     - Both procedures may result in discounts
   - Supplier's forms
     - Use of supplier's pre-printed or Web-based order forms
   - Standing order
   - Computerization
   - Alternative ways to cut costs

True/False

T F 1. The buying procedure is not complete until all products and services are properly received, stored and issued to employees.

T F 2. The major disadvantage of a purchasing requisition system is it creates a great deal of paperwork for the supplier.

T F 3. The major differences between ordering procedures at large and small properties are the degree of formality and the presence or absence of a full-time buyer.

T F 4. Ordering is a buyer's effort to monitor suppliers from day to day to ensure that products and services arrive at the right time and in an acceptable condition.

T F 5. Standing orders traditionally minimize ordering costs and the need to prepare purchase orders.

T F 6. Traditionally, the purchase order is completed before the purchase requisition.

T F 7. In most hospitality organizations, line-level employees will fill out purchase requisitions when they need to order supplies.

T F 8.   If a hospitality operation's buyer orders an item on a regular basis, a purchase requisition is unnecessary.

T F 9.   The Levinson approach to ordering is not usually used in operations that have a sophisticated computerized record-keeping and control systems.

T F 10. Across the hospitality industry, there is one template for a purchase order that is traditionally used.

Fill-in-the-Blank

1.   A _____ lists items or services that a particular department head needs.

2.   The _____ is the most common way for a buyer to determine the appropriate order size.

3.   The _____ or _____ (acronym) form restricts the overall amount that a buyer can purchase.

4.   _____ is most often used, at least in the hospitality industry, when purchasing furniture, fixtures, and equipment.

5.   _____ is the process of ordering enough miscellaneous items to preclude, for example, weekly ordering.

6.   Typically, a _____ is used in the hospitality industry whenever a manager or supervisor needs an item that the buyer does not order regularly.

7.   If an item is kept in a separate storage facility, the employee usually needs to complete a _____ and give it to the storeroom manager in exchange for the item.

8.   Purchased product normally follows a chain of operating activities that begins with _____.

9.   Large operations usually have at least one full-time _____ who is deeply involved in the purchasing function.

10. Unless an approved supplier has a specific requirement, _____ at the hospitality operation usually decides which ordering procedure to use.

Multiple Choice

1.   All of the following are disadvantages of purchase requisition systems except:
     a. the potential for backdoor selling
     b. too many people may be involved in deciding types and qualities of products
     c. the time and effort required to implement and operate purchase requisition systems
     d. most hospitality employees are not computer literate and may be unable to use the purchasing requisition system

2. To calculate par stock, the buyer or user-buyer must note what is on hand in the main storeroom areas and in the department areas and _____ what is on hand from the par stock, then _____ products needed for banquets or other special occasions.
   a. subtract, subtract
   b. add, add
   c. subtract, add
   d. none of the above

3. A _____ is generally a procedure whereby you set par stocks and the supplier's route salesperson, who might come to your place twice a week, leaves just enough product to bring you up to par.
   a. standing order
   b. back order
   c. filler order
   d. expedited order

4. All the following are benefits associated with a purchase requisition system except:
   a. it is useful training device for department heads who aspire to become full time   buyers
   b. it can relieve a buyer of responsibility for ordering mistakes
   c. it can relieve the buyer of all purchasing paperwork
   d. it is a way of controlling the use of products and services in the various departments

5. _____ is a method a buyer can use to place an order:
   a. fax
   b. e-mail
   c. telephone
   d. all of the above

6. At minimum, purchase order records should exist so that:
   a. they can be used as a comparison for delivery accuracy
   b. bills can be paid
   c. par stocks can be created for future orders
   d. employees can be trained on how to fill our PO's correctly

7. Small hospitality operations commonly follow _____ procedures that help to minimize the ordering effort.
   a. par stock
   b. one-stop shopping
   c. computerized ordering
   d. employee empowerment

8. A purchase order usually contains all of the following except:
   a. quantity desired
   b. item type
   c. unit price
   d. internal payment information

9. Traditionally, expediting is used in the hospitality industry when purchasing all of the following except:
   a. furniture
   b. fixtures
   c. food
   d. equipment

10. Even when a hospitality operation has a/an _____ policy, someone still must keep a close eye on what employees remove from the storeroom.
    a. open storeroom
    b. par stock policy
    c. e-purchasing
    d. anti-backdoor selling

Apply Your Knowledge
1. Explain three of the benefits associated with using an e-procurement application.

2. List and explain one procurement cost-cutting method.

Chapter 14
Typical Receiving Procedures
After reading this chapter, you should be able to
- Explain the objectives of receiving.
- Explain the essentials of effective receiving.
- Describe invoice receiving and other receiving methods.
- Outline additional receiving duties.
- List receiving practices and methods that reduce receiving costs.

Outline
1. Introduction
   - Receiving determines what you actually received (not necessarily what you ordered)
   - Receiving is the act of inspecting and accepting or rejecting deliveries
   - Wide range of receiving practices
2. The Objectives of Receiving
   - Similar to objectives of purchasing
   - Additional objective – to control received products and services
     o Cycle of control – where do items go after they are received
     o Receiving sometimes under direction of accounting department for additional control
3. Essentials for Receiving
   - Competent personnel
     o Appropriate training
       ▪ Recognize various quality levels of merchandise
       ▪ Be able to complete paperwork
       ▪ Know what to do in non-typical situations
   - Proper receiving equipment
     o Accurate scales for confirming weights (bare minimum)
     o Temperature probes for refrigerated or frozen foods
     o Rulers for checking trim of fat on steaks for example
     o Calculator for verifying cost
     o Knife for sampling
     o Conveyor belts, hand trucks and/or motorized lifts for moving purchases
     o Bar code reader
   - Proper receiving facilities
     o Well lit
     o Large enough to work in
     o Reasonably secure
     o Convenient for drivers and receivers
   - Appropriate receiving hours
   - Copies of all specifications
   - Copies of purchase orders
4. Invoice receiving
   - Delivery arrives
     o Invoice or bill accompanies the delivery
     o Receiving person checks quantity, quality and price of each item, confirming with the original purchase order
     o If no invoice accompanies the order, the receiving person will usually create one
     o Some operations require that buyer approve all substitutions, if there is a substitution buyer will be called
     o Creates time lag

- o Product could deteriorate or be destroyed by waiting (frozen foods)
- o Quality control or assurance inspectors often employed by large operations – inspect both purchases and products created (as in a commissary) – usually do not report to the buyer thus adding another level of control
- o If there is an issue buyer should be notified who will, in turn, notify supplier immediately
- o After quality has been verified, receivers usually check prices and price extensions plus sales and other applicable taxes
- o If delivery is acceptable, it is stored or delivered to the appropriate department
- Rejection of delivery
  - o Receiver may note discrepancy in price or taxes
  - o If product has been rejected, receiver may write a Request for Credit memorandum that would be signed by the driver
  - o Request for Credit may also be written if substitutions have been received – they are sometimes lower in price than the products originally requested
  - o The supplier issues the credit memo and the buyer's accounting department pays the invoice less the credit memo amount
  - o In other cases, the supplier will credit the amount on the next delivery
  - o In still other cases, drivers may have authority to "reprice" an invoice on the spot
  - o Being too picky and rejecting products too quickly is not always a good idea
    - ▪ Suppliers don't like buyers who send back reasonable substitutes
    - ▪ Rejecting an item means you may run short
- Returning merchandise
  - o Supplier gives driver "pick-up" memorandum
  - o Pick-up memo is left with receiver and serves as a receipt for the returned goods
- Acceptance of delivery
  - o Receiver usually signs delivery sheet or invoice
  - o Items are stored or delivered to appropriate departments
  - o Receiver stamps invoice with list of "checks" that are to be made and a space for the initials of the responsible party
  - o Receiver may record delivery on the receiving sheet
    - ▪ Receiving sheet usually contains redundant information
    - ▪ Forces receiver to re-record information and may bring mistakes to light
    - ▪ Provides record for evaluating supplier's performance
    - ▪ Useful to cost accounts when preparing certain reports
    - ▪ Comments column may contain information on the driver's attitude, cleanliness of the truck, etc.
    - ▪ Serves as a daily report of the receiver's actions
  - o Invoices, credit slips, the receiving sheet and bill of lading sent to the accounting department
  - o Storage area supervisor (if different from receiver) may get copy of receiving sheet as another type of control
- Additional receiving duties
  - o Date the delivered items
  - o Price all of the delivered items
  - o Create bar codes
  - o Apply meat tags
    - ▪ Contain two duplicate parts
    - ▪ During receiving, one part is put on the item and the other is sent to accounting
    - ▪ When item moves from storage to production, second tag is sent to accounting where the item is moved from inventory

- Units of measure on the meat tags should correspond to those used in production and the amounts sold to customers
  - o Housekeeping
  - o Update AP prices
  - o Backhaul recyclables
5. Other Receiving Methods
   - Standing-order receiving
     - o Delivery tickets rather than invoices may accompany the delivery
     - o Best to use invoice receiving to ensure that receivers, drivers and bill payers don't grow careless
   - Blind receiving
     - o Usually has item names only on invoice (no quantity or price information)
     - o Sometimes shipments come in with no invoice;
       - Receiver will confirm with management that item were order
       - Receiver will complete in-house invoice slip
     - o Odd-hours receiving
       - Regular receiver usually not available
       - Often conducted in a rush since stand-in for receiver probably has other duties
     - o Drop-shipment receiving
       - Main difference between drop-shipment receiving and invoice receiving is that the driver works for a third-party carrier and thus is not involved in any disputes regarding the merchandise (unless he/she damaged the merchandise in transit)
       - Buyer may be required to accept shipment even though it may be unacceptable, and then pay the shipping to have the products returned
       - Third-party insurance companies may need to inspect the merchandise in a dispute
     - o Mailed deliveries
       - Usually come with packing slips
       - Management usually handles requests for credit memos in case of an error
     - o Cash-on-delivery (COD) Deliveries
6. Good Receiving Practices
   - Should beware of excess ice, watered-down products or anything else that could add weight to a product
   - Should always check the quality of items under the top layer
   - Should always inspect packages for leakage or other water damage; swollen cans should be rejected
   - Should ensure that expiration date has not come and gone
   - Each item type should be weighed separately; e.g., ground beef should not be weighed with steak
   - Should be wary of drivers who are especially eager to help unload
   - Should not sign for incomplete orders even with the promise that the other materials are coming later, because later may never come
   - Should spot-check portions for proportion weights
   - Should be careful of closed shipping containers with expiration dates, weights, counts, etc.; might be good to occasionally open and count the napkins
   - Must not accept re-frozen merchandise
   - Must be careful to not confuse brand names or packers' brands
   - Should test for acceptable shrinkage
   - Adequate specifications must be prepared ahead of time so receivers can appropriately judge merchandise

- Make sure you don't get "stung" by drivers
  - Unintentional error
  - Dishonest supplier/honest driver
  - Honest supplier/dishonest driver
  - Dishonest supplier/dishonest driver
7. Reducing Receiving Costs
   - Field inspectors
   - Night and early-morning deliveries
   - One-stop shopping

True/False

T F 1. The buyer usually sends out the credit memo.

T F 2. A supplier's delivery person leaves a bill of lading for the receiver.

T F 3. One way to reduce receiving costs is to request that your supplier exclusively use third-party or common delivery companies.

T F 4. One must be careful to not falsely accuse someone of being dishonest. When there are regular occurrences of dishonesty, a buyer should realize that it could be the fault of the supplier, the driver or the shipper or any combination thereof.

T F 5. A supplier who consistently wants to make odd-hour deliveries on short notice might bear watching. He or she might know that the trained receiver is not working at those times and be trying to slip something by the inexperienced employee on the dock, such as a grade of beef that wasn't requested or fresh produce that is close to spoiling.

T F 6. The shrink allowance is the same as the tare weight.

T F 7. A price extension is the figure representing the number of items ordered multiplied by the price of the item. This figure should appear on invoices.

T F 8. It would be inappropriate for a receiver to slice open an apple or two from a case to make sure it is not rotten.

T F 9. The dot system can be used when dating and pricing items that are delivered.

T F 10. Quality assurance inspectors usually work for the buyer and are part of the cycle of control.

Fill-in-the-Blank

1. A common-carrier driver with an empty truck who picks up materials for recycling or perhaps even picks up an item that was drop-shipped and needs to be returned is _____.

2. The _____ is a usually redundant listing of the deliveries received. However, it can contain information about the driver that should not necessarily be included on an invoice.

3. _____ is the process for receiving an order that stays the same time after time. _____ is one of the dangers of such an order.

4.   A driver who is to load returned product after making a delivery at an operation is usually given a _____ by the supplier.

5.   An item that has been _____ was originally frozen but has been thawed so it can be sold as "fresh."

6.   When a receiver looks at produce, for example, that is not on the top of a case, he or she is ensuring that the contents are _____, and no damaged produce is hidden underneath.

7.   When older products are used first it is known as _____.

8.   _____ are a somewhat archaic but effective means of ensuring that expensive items, such as steaks, are accounted for until they go into production. They are similar to _____, which are requests from a department for specific items that are held in storage.

9.   Once an item is delivered it may not weigh as much as it did when it left the supplier's warehouse due to dehydration or other factors. The buyer takes this into account and has a tolerance level for this known as the _____.

10.   Receivers should make sure the _____ of a product is within acceptable limits, meaning that it should be fresh until a certain date.

Multiple Choice
1.   Which of the following is not true of a drop shipment?
      a. buyer may have to arrange for a common carrier to return merchandise if damaged
      b. shipment may be insured by an independent company and a representative may need to inspect the claim
      c. driver is not responsible for the product beyond any damage he or she might have caused
      d. accepting a common carrier shipment requires different receiving procedures

2. Which of the following practices is used to strengthen control within a purchasing system?
      a. blind receiving
      b. drop-shipping
      c. odd-hours receiving
      d. none of the above

3. Which of the following is not a step in accepting a shipment?
      a. delivery arrives
      b. receiver inspects materials
      c. receiver returns at least a portion of each order to keep supplier honest
      d. receiver stores materials

4.   Which of the following would not normally be a task of a receiver?
      a. adding barcodes to items
      b. negotiating with the supplier for different delivery times
      c. checking the invoice against the purchase order (P.O.)
      d. rejecting all or part of a delivery

5.   A buyer might use all of the following methods for ensuring that the products delivered meet the company's quality requirements except:
    a. training the receiver to estimate product weights
    b. refusing to accept odd-hour deliveries
    c. providing receiver with specifications sheets
    d. hiring a field inspector

6.   A quick visual inspection will most likely reveal which of the following?
    a. items that have been slacked out
    b. water damage
    c. items the supplier picked up at an auction
    d. none of the above

7.   If the acceptable trim amount is exceeded, which of the following can happen?
    a. the EP price goes up
    b. the AP price goes up
    c. the cost to the consumer goes up
    d. both "a" and "b" above

8.   One-stop shopping would most likely result in which of the following?
    a. lowered receiving costs
    b. lower AP costs
    c. erratic delivery schedules
    d. too many product options

9.   A buyer should re-think the relationship with a supplier if he or she consistently receives:
    a. incomplete shipments
    b. damaged merchandise
    c. items with more than the agreed upon trim amount
    d. all of the above

10. If a receiver gets a shipment without an invoice slip, he or she will most likely:
    a. call the buyer
    b. create a document to serve as the invoice
    c. call the accounting department
    d. refuse acceptance of the delivery

Apply Your Knowledge
1.   If you are on a COD basis and a supplier consistently delivers shipments that have something wrong with them—shipment contains items that weren't ordered, items are shorted, etc.—how would you deal with this? Would you be suspicious that your supplier is perhaps a bit less than honest?

2.   List and discuss all of the reasons a manager might want to continue the practice of having a receiver complete a delivery sheet.

Chapter 15
Typical Storage Management Procedures
After reading this chapter, you should be able to

- Explain the objectives of storage.
- Identify space, temperature, humidity, and other requirements of proper storage.
- Describe the process of managing storage facilities, including inventory.
- List important storage-management practices for small hospitality operators.

Outline
1. Introduction
   - "Storage" and "receiving" often go hand-in-hand
   - Items sent directly to a production area are known as direct purchases or directs
   - The person who receives is often the one who stores
   - Good control dictates some separation of responsibilities if possible
2. The Objectives of Storage
   - Prevent loss of merchandise
     o Theft
       ▪ Premeditated
       ▪ Prevented by
         • Clear visibility of storage area
         • Locked storerooms
         • Minimizing the number of persons with access
     o Pilferage
       ▪ Employee thieving
       ▪ Employees eating on the job (if not allowed)
       ▪ Referred to as inventory shrinkage or skimming
     o Spoilage
       ▪ Prevented by
         • Adherence to sanitation practices
         • Stock rotation
         • Providing proper environmental conditions for all products
       ▪ Can result in a company's loss of reputation
3. What is Needed to Achieve Storage Objectives
   - Adequate space
     o 5 square feet per dining seat (on average)
     o 15 square feet per hotel room (on average)
     o 10-12 percent of the total property (on average)
   - Adequate temperature and humidity
     o National Restaurant Association Educational Foundation (NRAEF) guidelines
       ▪ Meat, poultry, fresh fish, processed crustaceans, dairy products, reduced oxygen packaged foods, some ready-to-eat foods prepared in-house: 41°F or lower
       ▪ Live shellfish, eggs: 45°F or lower
       ▪ Fruits and vegetables: 41°F to 70°F
       ▪ Dry and canned food: 50°F to 70°F
       ▪ Freezer storage: 0°F to 10°F
     o Storage requirements
       ▪ 4" from walls and ceilings
       ▪ 6" off the floor
       ▪ Non-solid shelving for air circulation
       ▪ Foods cannot be stored under any unprotected sewer or water lines

- Foods cannot be stored in rooms with garbage or toilet facilities
- Soaps, chemicals and pest control supplies must be stored in separate storage areas from foods
  - Adequate equipment
    - Shelving/racks
    - Trucks
    - Covered containers
  - Proximity of storage area to receiving and production areas
  - Access to proper maintenance (repair of freezers)
  - Proper security
  - Competent personnel to supervise and manage storage function
  - Sufficient time to perform the necessary duties
  - Storeroom regulations for control and predictability
    - Who is allowed to enter storage areas
    - Required procedure for obtaining items
4. Managing the Storage Facilities
  - Small operations usually don't have many controls in place
  - Liquor storage is the exception
  - Storeroom manager's possible duties
    - Classify inventories and organize in a systematic fashion
    - Determine usage rates for all inventories
    - Make or pick-up an emergency order
    - Keep track of accumulating surpluses
    - Be responsible for disposing of items
    - Manage transfers of merchandise to other company outlets
    - Keep track of all inventories and dollar values
      - Perpetual inventory
        - Could include in-process inventories
        - Generally reserved for expensive items
        - Bin card records for liquor or other items
          - Items received
          - Sent to production
          - Returned to storage (if applicable)
        - Provides for tight control
        - Requires computerized management information system (MIS)
      - Physical Inventory
        - Conducted on regular basis (weekly, monthly, etc.)
        - Three reasons for physical counting of inventory
          - Helps with calculating order sizes
          - Necessary for accounting department when calculating product costs
          - In cases where perpetual inventory is used, can be a good "check"
        - Time consuming – but less so than maintaining perpetual inventory
        - Minimum of once a month to provide information for monthly profit-and loss statement
        - Several methods exist
          - Two person – one writing, one calling out figures
          - Use of a handheld bar code scanner

- o Count everything in the warehouse, add predetermined percentage to represent amount in process
- o Count only full-case equivalents
- o Combining ordering with inventory taking
- o Use a tape recorder to recite counts and have someone transcribe the information
- o Use a handheld computer device to encode inventories
- Control options
  - o Representative of accounting or some other department conducts inventory
  - o Have head bartender take inventory of food storage area and the chef inventory the liquor
  - o Hire an outside service
- Exercising tight control over the stock
  - Allow only a few persons to withdraw items from storeroom
  - Perhaps the most important part of a storeroom manager's job
  - Maintain small stock so pilferage is more noticeable
  - Use small working storerooms and keep large storerooms locked
  - Use stock requisition system
  - Have the accounting department responsible for issues
  - Issue stock only at certain terms during the day
  - Issue exact amounts of ingredients for one day or one shift

5. A Value Analysis of Storage Management Procedures
   - Operations can theoretically capture a 2 percent savings from optimal storage management procedures
   - Large operators can afford additional personnel – and the savings is greater
   - Small operators do have economical options
     - o Use one-stop shopping
     - o Have owner-manager or assistant receive and inspect all incoming merchandise; send expensive items to the main storage area and less expensive items to production
     - o Have the owner-manager issue par stocks of the expensive items to users at the beginning of their shifts
     - o Lock main storage facilities
     - o Have owner-manager retrieve additional expensive items as needed during shifts
     - o Have owner-manager open main storage area to re-stock unused expensive items
     - o Have owner-manager record expensive items used during the shift and pass information on to bookkeeper who will compare what was used with what was sold (critical-item inventory analysis)

True/False

T F 1. Theft, pilferage, inventory shrinkage and skimming are terms that all mean the same thing.

T F 2. Taking a physical inventory is less time-consuming than maintaining a perpetual inventory.

T F 3. In some manual inventory-taking methods, it is permissible to skip over partially used or open items and count only full boxes, cases or cans.

T F 4. Critical item inventory analyses are of great value when they are conducted on a sporadic basis.

T F 5. A company wanting to exercise greater control over the inventory might have the chef perform the liquor inventory and the head bartender perform the food and supplies inventory.

T F 6. In a small operation, the owner-manager's participation in the storage and issuing process can dramatically cut down on pilfering.

T F 7. In a medium-sized operation where the receiver, stocker and storeroom manager is the same person, additional controls are unnecessary as this person has all the information he or she needs.

T F 8. Health district storage temperature requirements are usually much more stringent than those established by the National Restaurant Association Educational Foundation.

T F 9. A perpetual inventory is considered to be "theoretical" because it is a calculated figure and doesn't include a physical count of the items.

T F 10. Control and security are considered to be the most important aspects of a storeroom manager's job.

Fill-in-the-Blank

1. _____ is a national trade association that has published guidelines for optimum storage temperatures.

2. A _____ is a formal request for an item that helps management control inventory. It records who received the items, how much was distributed and when the items were issued

3. A recording of the number of expensive items that were used during a shift and comparing that number with the sales records is known as _____, _____ or _____.

4. Items, that when received are sent directly to the kitchen for immediate use rather than first being placed in storage are known as _____ or _____.

5. _____ and _____ are two environmental factors that need to be taken into consideration when designing storage areas.

6. An _____ is a place where ingredients for restaurant offerings are measured and issued on a daily or shift basis. A similar area is called the _____ where only small amounts of product are available to employees and the main warehouse space is kept locked and is available only to management personnel.

7. The standard system for providing stock to chefs, housekeepers and bartenders is known as _____.

8. An operation's food costs equals _____.

9. A _____ is required to effectively maintain a perpetual inventory.

10. One of the first tasks of the storeroom manager is to _____ and _____ the items.

Multiple Choice

1. Which of the following might not aid inventory control in a small operation?
   a. maintaining a working storeroom
   b. maintaining a minimal inventory
   c. having specific hours of operation for the storeroom
   d. utilizing multiple suppliers

2. A manager-owner who wants to speed up the inventory process might do which of the following?
   a. use a perpetual inventory system
   b. use a tape recorder to record the figures and transcribe the information
   c. maintain a small amount of inventory at all times
   d. answers "b" and "c" above

3. Buyers will receive the most benefit from which of the following storeroom manager's activities?
   a. calculation of inventory usage rates
   b. classifying and organizing inventory items
   c. maintaining a clean storage area
   d. issuing products to users

4. Which of the following would not normally be a task of the storeroom manager?
   a. organizing the storeroom
   b. checking the invoice against the purchase order (P.O.)
   c. keeping track of accumulating surpluses
   d. picking up an emergency order

5. Which of the following might be included in the inventory-taking process?
   a. head bartender
   b. accountant
   c. outside service
   d. all of the above

Apply Your Knowledge

1. In other chapters we discussed the importance of buying products at the right price, in the right amount, at the right time. Discuss the impact the possibility of "spoilage" will have on these purchasing factors.

2. One-stop shopping, although perhaps not the best method for achieving the optimum AP price, has been touted as saving money in relation to ordering and receiving costs. Now in this chapter, one-stop shopping is being suggested as a possible way for small operators to control inventories. Discuss one-stop shopping in light of all of these factors taking into consideration the pros and cons associated with each.

Chapter 16
Security in the Purchasing Function
After reading this chapter, you should be able to:
- Describe the security problems associated with the purchasing function.
- Identify methods used to prevent security problems related to purchasing.

Outline
1. Introduction
   - Employees are stealing from their employers
   - Theft is no longer an issue of simply marking up the menu or room price to accommodate loses
   - The public has become more security conscious
   - Insurance costs have gone up
   - Unfavorable publicity has focused on hospitality purchasing practices
   - Buyers can enforce a good measure of security within their realm of responsibility
2. Security problems
   - Kickbacks
     - Example: hospitality company could pay for superior item, receive inferior item and the cost difference would be split between salesperson and buyer
     - Example: padding the invoice-phony charges added to an invoice
     - Example: invoice is sent to bookkeeping twice and conspirators pocket the second payment
     - Example: buyer agrees to pay a slightly higher AP price and receives an under-the-table payment from the supplier
   - Invoice scams: diverting a bill payment to a fictitious company
   - Supplier and receiver error
     - Arithmetic errors on the invoice
     - Other errors
       - Losing credit for container deposits or returned merchandise
       - Receiving substitute item and failing to issue a Request for Credit memo
       - Receiving the wrong items intentionally
       - Weighing items with an inaccurate scale
   - Inventory theft
     - Access to storage should be limited
   - Inventory padding
     - A food supervisor might want to increase or "pad" the ending inventory so food costs appear lower than they really are
   - Inventory substitutions
     - Employees might remove high-quality merchandise and substitute inferior goods
   - Telephone and e-mail sales scams
     - Offers of sweet deals on products
     - Payments made for unauthorized shipments are seldom recouped
   - Inability to segregate operating activities
     - Ideal setup—different people for buying, receiving, storing and bill-paying procedures
     - When buyer also receives, opens door to security issues
     - Buyers receive for several reasons
       - They are the only who recognize various product quality standards
       - Buyers must do other things to justify time on the job
       - Management cannot afford to hire a separate receiver
   - Suspicious behavior

- Owner managers should be wary of employees who:
  - Seem unduly friendly with salespeople
  - Hand around storage areas
  - Needlessly handle keys or locks
  - Make too many trips to garbage areas
  - Requisition abnormally large amounts of supplies
  - Make frequent trips to the storage areas for no real reason
  - Have relatives working for the suppliers
  - Frequently stray from assigned workstations
  - Are seen stuffing boxes or packages under a couch
  - Permit drivers to loiter in unauthorized areas
  - Have visitors on the work site
3. Preventing Security Problems
   - Three steps to preventing security breaches
     - Select honest suppliers
     - Employ honest employees
     - Design physical facilities to ensure effective security conditions
   - Ask other operators about suppliers' honesty
   - Employers are beginning to prosecute dishonest employees and customers
   - Effective recruiting and selection procedure is good weapon against employee theft
     - Background investigations
     - Integrity tests
     - Reference checks
   - Secure design of facilities is easy in new-builds or major remodels
   - In existing buildings, owner-manager may have to deal with things as they are
   - The following will help prevent theft:
     - Document cash paid-outs
     - Never pay an invoice that shows a post office box number as the supplier's address
     - Those who buy should never pay the bills
     - Owner-manager should cancel paperwork on all completed transactions (and make sure it has been completed in the case of returned merchandise that needs to be credited to the operation's account)
       - Bill payers should compare invoice with original purchase order
       - AP prices, delivery charges and other costs should be compared with those quoted earlier
     - Arrange for independent auditors to do the following:
       - Analyze invoices and payment checks
       - Check receiving routine and equipment
       - Inspect storage facilities
       - Check receiving sheets and stock requisitions for consistency with invoices, purchase orders and payment checks
       - Check consumption against reported sales
       - Audit coupons
     - Employ spotters or shoppers
     - Implement the use of integrity or personality tests and drug tests
     - Employ a fidelity bonding company
     - Consider using a trash compactor
     - Designate an employees-only entrance
     - Designate an employee parking area away from the building
     - Employee locker rooms should be close enough for manager to check occasionally

- o Drivers should not be allowed to loiter
- o Receivers should not be rushed
- o Only employees and other authorized personnel should be in the back of the house
- o Invest in cost-effective physical barriers
    - Time locks
    - Heavy-duty locks
    - Adequate lighting in storage areas
    - Closed-circuit television or digital video recorders
    - Uniformed guards
    - See-through screens on storage facility doors
    - Perimeter and interior alarm systems
- o Separate the buying, receiving, storing and issuing activities and even separate the bill-paying function from the bookkeeping
- o Compare AP prices of other suppliers
- o Try not to hire employees who have relatives working for suppliers
- o Ensure that bill payer checks bills carefully
- o Everything should be removed from the shipping container before storing it
- o Be leery of cash deposits
- o Become a house account for one or more trusted suppliers
- o Develop a system to prevent unrecorded merchandise from getting into the storage facilities or in-process inventory
- o Do not order inadequate products from phone solicitors and others
- o Develop an approved supplier list
- o Avoid purchasing merchandise in small, single-service packages
- o Restrict access to all high-cost products
- o Owner-manager should maintain close watch on all expensive items
- o Adopt technology to calculate theoretical-inventory value
- o Ensure that access to records is restricted
- o Owner-manager must be concerned with security precautions in other parts of the operation
- • Owner manager will be one of two minds:
    - o Security will become a mania
    - o Security will occupy a low position on the priority list
4. Who Checks the Checker
    - • Impossible to have a complete set of checks and balances
    - • An adequate management information system should help monitor purchasing-receiving-storage cycle

True/False

T F 1.   In today's age of video technology and recent federal legislation, employee theft is no longer a serious issue in the hospitality industry.

T F 2.   As long as others within the company are doing the same, purchasing agents are allowed to accept gifts and other economic favors from suppliers.

T F 3.   In actuality, the honest supplier is the loser if salespersons or drivers conspire with receivers, buyers, or bookkeepers.

T F 4.   The larger the operation, the more unlikely it is to be victim of an invoice scam.

T F 5.   The employee entrance door should not be used to receive deliveries.

T F 6. When a choice is available, it is better to pay for deliveries with cash, not a check.

T F 7. The victim in phone scams is always the authorized purchasing agent.

T F 8. Buyers should always be permitted to pay bills of the hospitality organization

T F 9. An operation should use the receiving area as a designated employee smoking area.

T F 10. Compared to the other operational challenges, theft, fraud, pilferage, and shoplifting are only minor problems.

Fill-in-the-Blank

1. _____ an invoice is when two or more conspirators add on a phony charge.

2. A _____ is the term given to the scenario where a buyer/user-buyer colludes with a supplier, salesperson, or driver.

3. To reduce theft, only _____ should be granted access to storage and receiving facilities.

4. Hospitality operators have trouble with pilferage because many of the products can easily be converted into _____.

5. A _____ is an individual who poses as a customer to observe pertinent operational activities within the organization.

6. A _____ insures a hospitality company against employee theft of cash.

7. An _____ occurs when someone diverts a bill payment to a fictitious company.

8. _____ occurs when an employee removes high-quality merchandise and replaces it with inferior goods.

9. Because it is relatively inexpensive, as well as difficult to trace, _____ are becoming popular for scamming hospitality operators.

10. Lately, more hospitality organizations are beginning to _____ dishonest employees and dishonest customers. This stern action should help minimize the number of dishonest people who are employed at hospitality enterprises.

Multiple Choice

1. According to Ernst & Young, one in every _____ employees is apprehended for theft from his or her employer each year.
   a. 27
   b. 17
   c. 37
   d. 7

2. Heightened interest in security is due to all of the following except:
   a. difficult to pass on security losses to the consumer
   b. the public has become more rigorous in its security precautions
   c. more restaurants are now becoming publicly traded operations
   d. the cost of insurance coverage has dramatically increased

3. An owner-manager can take all the following steps to prevent security breaches except:
   a. personally overseeing every tiny detail of the operation
   b. employ honest employees
   c. select honest suppliers
   d. ensure his or her operation facilities have effective security conditions

4. _____ is a hospitality operator's main weapon in the fight against employee theft and pilferage.
   a. constant employee training
   b. an open door policy
   c. personnel recruiting and selection
   d. an armed security force

5. Each year, the foodservice industry loses approximately _____ due to theft and cash mishandling.
   a. $20 million
   b. $2 million
   c. $2 billion
   d. $20 billion

6. The most common type of kickback happens when the buyer agrees to:
   a. pay a slightly higher AP price and receives a kickback from the supplier
   b. forge the appropriate signatures on purchase orders
   c. use a supplier where a member of his or her family works
   d. chooses to receive the wrong product from the supplier

7. Buyers who also serve the operation as a receiver are common in the hospitality industry for all the following reasons except:
   a. they are the only ones who can recognize product quality standards
   b. there is a shortage of trained receivers in the hospitality industry
   c. the buyer must do other things to justify time on the job
   d. management can not afford to hire a separate receiver

8. _____ tests are thought to be one of the most effective weapons in the war against theft and pilferage.
   a. supervision
   b. open Book
   c. performance
   d. integrity

9. Dishonest employees steal almost _____ times the amount stolen by shoplifters
   a. 18
   b. 28
   c. 8
   d. 38

10. The most common type of inventory shrinkage is _____.
     a. pilferage by employee
     b. drivers dropping of incorrect quantities
     c. spoilage
     d. comp meals due to guest inconvenience

Apply Your Knowledge
1. Discuss three examples of suspicious behavior in the receiving area and think about how you might approach an employee who is exhibiting this behavior and what you would say to him or her.

2. Discuss three methods to increase security in the purchasing function.

Chapter 17
Fresh Produce
After reading this chapter, you should be able to:
- Explain the selection factors for fresh produce, including government grades.
- Explain the process of purchasing, receiving, storing and issuing fresh produce.

Outline
1. Introduction
   - Purchasing fresh produce requires skill and knowledge
   - Some operations hire professional produce buyers
   - Fresh-produce buyers are extremely well paid
   - Savvy buyers will subscribe to related trade publications
   - Several hundred varieties of fresh produce items are available
   - Buyers may experience a lack of acceptable sources
2. Selection factors
   - Owner-manager usually specifies quality levels of fresh produce
   - Owner-manager works with others to determine quality standards as well as the preferred supplier
     - Intended use
     - Exact name
     - U.S. Government Inspection and Grades (or equivalent)
       - First standard for fresh produce was for potatoes (1917)
       - U.S. No. 1 was given to the highest grade
       - U.S. No. 2 was given to remainder of the crop for sale under normal conditions
       - U.S. Inspection Service for fresh produce was established same year
       - Perishable Agricultural Commodities Act was signed in 1930, prohibiting unfair and fraudulent practices in interstate commerce of fruits and vegetables
       - Agricultural Marketing Act (1946)
         - Provided for integrated administration of marketing programs
         - Gave Agricultural Marketing Service (AMS) authority including federal standards, grading and inspection services, market news services, market expansion and consumer education
       - Grade standards for 150 fruits vegetables and nuts
       - Each vegetable or fruit might have a different grading system
       - Buyers need information on grades
         - USDA
         - PMA Fresh Produce Manual
       - Appearance is the most important factor
         - Size
         - Uniformity
         - Maturity
         - Shape
         - Color
         - Texture
         - Freedom from disease, decay, cuts and bruises
       - Produced shipped long distances may have more stringent examination to ensure that it represents the grade stated at the delivery point
         - Wise buyer will insist that fruit/vegetables meet specified grade at time of delivery

- Grading terms
  - Fancy: top quality; about 1% of all produce
  - No. 1: bulk of items; grade most purchased
  - Commercial: slightly lower quality than No. 1
  - No. 2: Much lower quality that No. 1; very superior to U.S. No. 3
  - Combination: usually a mix of No. 1 and No. 2
  - No. 3: low-quality barely acceptable for packing
  - Field run: ungraded products
- Low-grade items end up in food-processing plants
- Grades are unavailable for some fresh produce
  - Not available for that item
  - Suppliers refuse to have item graded
  - Produce may come from a foreign country
- Grade is just one of many factors influencing buyers' decisions
  o Packers' brands (or equivalent)
- Not a lot of fresh-produce brands available
- Most prominent
  - Sunkist®
  - Chiquita®
  - Dole®
- May indicate a specific packing or cleaning process has been used
- Consistency is important
  - Results in a more predictable edible-portion (EP) cost
  - Helps minimize variation between and within case packs
- Packer may not purchase U.S. grading service, intermittent inspections are mandatory
  - A stenciled "No. 1" on a box indicates that the product is not under continual government inspection, nor has it been graded, but in the opinion of the packer it meets all requirements for this grade
- Packers sometimes put out two categories under the same brand
  o Product Size
- Important for several reasons
  - Embarrassing to serve guests items of varying sizes
  - If products were sold by piece rather than weight, effective cost control would be impossible
- Count per box is one measure
- Number of pieces per layer or lug (box) is another measure
  - A 4 x 5 indicates a layer of four items on one side and five on the other or 20 per layer
- Some products have a nomenclature
  - Pre-pack
  - Large medium
  - Jumbo
  - Colossal
- Number of pieces per pound is another measure: 3 to 1 indicates three items per pound
  o Size of container
  o Type of packaging material

- Packaging procedure
  - Layered
    - Individually wrapped
    - Cell-packed
  - Slab-packed
- Minimum weight per case
- Product yield
- Point of origin
- Color
- Product form
- Degree of Ripeness
- Ripening process used
- Preservation method
  - Refrigeration
  - Waxing
  - Controlled-atmosphere storage
    - Oxygen is removed and other gasses introduced
    - Oxidize or remove the ethylene gas
  - Chemically treated
- Trusting the supplier

3. Purchasing Fresh Produce
   - Obtain PMA Fresh Produce Manual
   - Decide on exact type of produce and quality required
   - Prepare specifications for each item
   - Consider available suppliers (bid-buying not as prevalent for fresh produce as it is for processed foods and nonfood items)
   - Local farmers may be a good idea
     - Some "farmers" may purchase produce from another source
     - Not likely to be inspected
   - Some operators may have their own gardens

4. Receiving Fresh Produce
   - Taking delivery of fresh produce is a challenge
     - Conduct a visual inspection of top layer
     - Conduct random inspection of remaining layers of package
     - Too zealous an inspection can damage product

5. Storing Fresh Produce
   - Frequent deliveries is one of the best answers
   - Must be stored immediately at the proper temperature
   - Buyers should research the best possible environment for each fruit and vegetable
   - Produce should not be washed before it is stored
   - Produce should only be handled when it is necessary

6. Issuing Fresh Produce
   - If items go to central-storage, owner may want to consider sending ready-to-go items to the kitchen, i.e., clean, chopped onions rather than whole onions
   - Proper stock rotation is important

7. In-Process Inventories
   - Supervision is required to ensure that salad greens do not sit out at room temperature for too long
   - Considerable avoidable loss is associated with fresh produce

True/False

T F 1.   In some situations, it is appropriate for hospitality operations to hire professional produce buyers to select and procure fresh produce.

T F 2.   Unfortunately, pay for a supply house produce buyer is very low.

T F 3.   The first grade standard in the U.S. for fresh produces was developed in 1917.

T F 4.   There is only one type of packaging material approved by the U.S. government for packing fresh-produce.

T F 5.   Generally, when a buyer specifies the type or variety of merchandise desired, that will indicate color.

T F 6.   In certain situations, hospitality operations may order and accept produce, even though it is not ripe.

T F 7.   A case of fresh-produce always stays the same weight while in transit to the hospitality operation.

T F 8.   Consistency helps to minimize the variation both between and within case packs.

T F 9.   Government grades are the sole method for buying fresh produce.

T F 10. The nice thing about produce is that there is no variety to fresh natural food product quality.

Fill-in-the-Blank

1.   Next to fresh _____ procurement, fresh produce buying is perhaps the most difficult purchasing task the hospitality buyer faces.

2.   There are several _____ varieties of fresh-produce items that are regularly available at any given time from various primary sources and intermediaries.

3.   A buyer must not only specify the type of fresh produce, but must also specify the _____.

4.   The grade most often ordered is the high end of U.S. _____ or the equivalent.

5.   Because branded fresh produce is not as commonplace as branded canned and frozen goods, some buyers use both U.S. government grades and _____ when developing their fresh-produce buying procedures.

6.   Buyers would find it impossible to achieve effective cost control if varying _____ of fresh produce are served.

7.   A tomato lug size of 4 x _____ contains 20 tomatoes per layer.

8.   Packaging of fresh-produce usually takes two forms: slab-packing merchandise and _____.

9. The application of _____ can prevent moisture loss and also contribute to the appearance of the produce.

10. By asking for _____ produce, a buyer desires produce that has been grown without the use of synthetic chemicals and fertilizers.

Multiple Choice
1. _____ has an impact on produce.
   a. geographical area
   b. soil
   c. seasons
   d. all of the above

2. The _____ usually specifies the quality levels of fresh produce desired.
   a. owner-manager
   b. buyer
   c. receiver
   d. chef

3. Currently, the _____ is responsible for the creation of the grading standards for approximately 150 types of fruits, vegetables, and nuts.
   a. FDA
   b. USDA
   c. AHLA
   d. ATF

4. When a U.S. government grader is grading fresh produce, the most important factor is:
   a. size
   b. appearance
   c. color
   d. location of growth

5. All of the following are grading terms used for fresh fruits, vegetables, and nuts except:
   a. gorgeous
   b. fancy
   c. No. 1
   d. field run

6. _____ can result in a much more predictable EP cost.
   a. size
   b. location of growth
   c. buyer experience
   d. consistency

7. _____ is an acceptable delivery temperature for chopped salad greens.
   a. 33°
   b. 34°
   c. 37°
   d. 38°

8.	The first step in the purchasing of fresh produce is to:
	a. create specifications
	b. obtain the PMA Fresh Produce Manual
	c. develop budget
	d. find suppliers

9.	The first step in receiving a produce shipment is to:
	a. make a visual inspection of the top layer of the carton
	b. pay the driver
	c. check the prices of the delivery
	d. provide driver with next purchase order.

10.	The designation for ungraded produce is:
	a. commercial
	b. organic
	c. field run
	d. hybrid

Apply Your Knowledge
1.	A product specification for a tomato could include color, size, ripeness and location of origin among other things. Write three menu items that would include two or more of these in the description.

2.	Name the U.S grades for fresh produce and think of a possible application for each in a restaurant.

Chapter 18
Processed Produce and Other Grocery Items
After reading this chapter, you should be able to:
- Identify management considerations surrounding the selection and procurement of processed produce and other grocery items.
- Identify the selection factors for processed produce and other grocery items, including government grades.
- Describer the process of purchasing, receiving, storing and issuing processed produce and other grocery items.

Outline
1. Introduction
   - Purchasing procedures for convenience items are more routine than those required for fresh products
   - Purchasing processed items requires several management decisions
     - What the operation wants
     - What products are best suited for its needs
     - Which suppliers can accommodate those needs
2. Management Considerations
   - Which products should be fresh and which should be processed?
   - Produce is processed for many reasons in addition to preserving and increasing shelf life
     - Smooth out seasonal taste fluctuations
     - Capture items at peak of flavor
   - Major decision is whether or not to use processed food at all
   - Must determine which processing method to use:
     - Dried
     - Refrigerated
     - Frozen
     - Pickling
     - Fermentation
     - Chemical Preservatives
   - The buyer's selection of a processing method is affected by:
     - Food quality
     - AP Price
     - Need for convenience
   - Management must also consider the question of substitution
   - Other management considerations
     - Neglecting generally accepted purchasing principles when purchasing processed goods.
     - Neglect may be nurtured by the cavalier attitude with which some employees approach inventory
     - Impulse purchases
     - New products
     - Buying one processed item may entail purchasing something else, such as equipment or special supplies
     - Opportunity buys, such as introductory offers, quantity discounts, volume discounts, salvage buys, etc.
     - Buyers must determine which container size to buy
     - Should buyers accept an offer that would involve changing the form of the product they usually purchase?

3. Selection Factors
   - Management decides the quality, type and style of food wanted for each processed item.
   - Intended use
   - Exact name
     o Buyers must become familiar with the market terminology
     o Government has issued "Standards of Identity" for food products
     o Some standards set specific processing requirements
     o Standards of identity available for approximately 235 items
   - US Government Inspection and Grades (or equivalent)
     o The USDA and FDA conduct mandatory inspections of processor's facilities
     o Government inspection is mandatory
     o Grading service is voluntary and food processors must pay for it
     o Buyers can specify that the products desired must carry the federal-government inspection shield
     o Federal grades have been established for canned, bottled, frozen and dried produce and grocery items
     o Grading factors include:
       - Color
       - Uniformity of size and shape
       - Number of defects and blemishes
       - Character (Texture, Tenderness and Aroma)
       - Quality of packing medium may also be important
         o Water
         o Brine
         o Syrup
     o Grading factors for frozen foods include:
       - Uniformity of size and shape
       - Maturity
       - Quality
       - Color
       - Number of defects and blemishes
     o Grading factors for dried foods include:
       - Uniformity of size and shape
       - Color
       - Number of blemishes and defects
       - Moisture content
       - The way products are packed
     o Buyers could rely on the following grading categories for canned, bottled, frozen and dried items:
       - Grade A
       - Grade B
       - Grade C
   - Packers' brands (or equivalent)
     o Buyers can sometimes be "coerced" into purchasing brand name products by tradition or customer demand
     o Many processed items come and go
     o Since packaging can be unstandardized, buyers may seek out brands that meet their particular packaging requirements

- o For some items a packer's brand may be the most important indication of quality and flavor
  - o Some buyers may be wary about trading one brand for another simply because they detect a slightly different flavor
  - o Some producers prepare several qualities under the same brand
  - o Buyers can also opt for generic brands
- Product size
  - o A very important consideration is the question of size or count
  - o In lieu of specifying the count, buyers can indicate by using terms such as "large", "extra large", "jumbo" or other appropriate term
  - o Buyers may also want to know how many cups they can get from a can or frozen pack
- Size of container
  - o The EP cost becomes the buyers' main consideration when they evaluate appropriate container sizes
- Type of packaging material
  - o For frozen and dried products, the packaging materials are not as standardized
  - o Ease of opening and closing for storage
    - Can it be opened easily and closed again for safe storage?
  - o Environmentally safe packaging
    - Can the container or pouch be recycled?
  - o Personalization
    - Can purchase items with logo's or other advertisements
    - May increase the AP price
    - Advertising advantage may outweigh the cost
- Packaging procedure
  - o Slab-packed (most items)
  - o Layered (most expensive)
  - o Pouch packaging
    - Offers greater flexibility
    - Advantages include:
      - o Labor savings
      - o Food safety
      - o Convenience
- Drained weight (servable weight)
  - o The weight of containers can vary
  - o Calculate "drained weight" when purchasing canned items
    - This is done by draining off juices or other fluids and measuring the weight of the remaining product
  - o Thaw frozen fruit and cook frozen vegetables before weighing them
  - o Be wary of purchasing anything after considering only the volume
    - Standard of fill
    - Pump air into the product
    - Lower specific gravity of the product
- Type of processing
- Color
- Product Form
- Packing Medium
  - o Water

- o Syrup
- o No added medium
- o "Brix" level
- o When purchasing vegetable products, buyers may be able to specify the type and amount of sauce desired
- The use of additives and preservatives
  - o Difficult and costly to get products without additives and preservatives
- Other information that may appear on a packaging label
  - o The federal government requires a great deal of information on consumer product labels
  - o Hospitality operators would be interested in additional information such as:
    - Packaging dates
    - Freshness dates
    - Serving cost data
  - o School foodservice buyers seek out products that carry Child Nutrition labels
  - o When food processors put these details on the package labels, buyers must expect to pay for the added value
- One-stop shopping opportunities
  - o Small operations tend to prefer one-stop shopping for many items
  - o National corporations carry extensive lines of processed produce to compete with local and regional distributors
  - o These companies control all aspects of production and distribution
  - o They typically offer only one level of product quality
  - o Their products are referred to as "controlled brands"
  - o Broadline distributors distribute many types of products as well as many different "packer's grades" in most product lines
  - o Large firms usually have the time to shop around and take advantage of opportunity buys
  - o One-stop shopping provides a subtle advantage
    - Shortages sometimes occur and being a good customer may ensure a buyer a continual supply
- AP price
  - o The EP cost is the only relevant concern for a buyer
  - o EP cost includes:
    - Cost of product
    - Cost of labor
    - Cost of energy
    - Other overhead expenses
  - o Since there are a number of varieties, styles, and packaging methods, there are different AP prices
  - o Since lower grades are acceptable in some recipes, lower qualities can be purchased to save money
  - o For similar items, a buyer usually pays similar AP prices; but some suppliers may give better quantity discounts and volume discounts than others
  - o Bid buying can save money, but only if a buyer is willing to accept a large supply, put the cash up front, and make the buy at new pack times
  - o Disadvantages of bid buying:
    - If a buyer is "locked in" for a year, the menu is somewhat set.
    - If AP prices for similar items fall, the buyer cannot take advantage of them when the storage area is full

- Supplier service
  - Canned products require only nominal supplier service
  - Frozen items are more perishable and require greater service
  - Buyers may want to obtain a stockless purchasing deal, in which they protect an AP price for six months to a year
  - Buyers would also like to receive reasonable "break points."
  - Only certain buyers may be on the list of those slated to get some of that supply.
    - Bid buyers may be left behind
    - House accounts find themselves in a better position than bid buyers.
  - Another service is the delivery schedule
    - Most buyers can live with weekly or bi-weekly delivery
- Local supplier or national source
  - Buyers can go to the primary source and have items drop-shipped
  - Can also buy direct and arrange for a local supplier to distribute the merchandise
4. Purchasing Processed Produce and Other Grocery Items
- First step: obtain copies of reference materials
- Determine precisely what to order.
- Determine ordering procedures
  - Day-to-day
    - Can make changes quickly
  - Long-term contract on a bid basis
    - If they purchase on a bid basis, they will need detailed specifications
- Before buyer signs a long-term contract, should examine bidders' products
  - Perform "can-cutting tests" on the competing products
  - Other cutting-tests
    - Always check frozen fruit after it has thawed
    - Cook frozen vegetables from the frozen state before testing them
    - Check canned goods immediately after opening them
    - Conduct tests of dried and concentrated products on the reconstituted product
- Buyers should test products after they have been prepared for customer service
- Buyers may want to prepare a full recipe with each competitors product and then perform their tests
5. Receiving Processed Produce and Other Grocery Items
- Generally accepted inspection procedures
  - Canned, bottled, and pouch products
    - Check containers for swelling, leaks, rust, dents or broken seals
  - Dried products
    - Check the condition of the containers; look for mold, broken pieces and odd appearance
  - Frozen products
    - Check the condition of the container, looking for indication of thawing and refreezing; stained packaging indicates this.
    - Check the food temperature
    - Check for freezer burn
  - Check for repacking
    - Receiver should open some packages to be sure they are receiving the items ordered
  - Carefully check incoming products against the invoice and a copy of the purchase order
  - Be careful of supplier substitutions

        o   After checking quality and quantity, check the prices and complete appropriate accounting documents
6. Storing Processed Produce and Other Grocery Items
   - Generally accepted procedures for storing processed products have also been established:
     - Canned and bottled products
       - Store in a dry area at approximately 50° to 70° F
       - Avoid fluctuation in temperature and humidity
       - Heat can be damaging
       - Avoid dampness
       - Keep all canned and bottled products tightly covered and open only what is necessary
     - Dried products
       - Be careful of dampness
       - Try to keep them cooler than canned items so that insects are not attracted to them
     - Frozen products
       - Store these products at -10° F or lower
       - Be careful not to damage any packages
       - Avoid fluctuations in temperature
   - Grocery items require different storage environments
   - Pay attention to proper stock rotation
   - Other storage considerations
     - Keep items off the floor
     - Try not to mix new products with old products
     - If possible, use bins that load from the top and unload from the bottom
7. Issuing Processed Produce and Other Grocery Items
   - Hospitality operators often find a good deal of neglect for may processed items
     - Such products as individual containers of catsup, salt and sugar
   - The best way to reduce waste is to ensure that written stock requisitions exist for every item and that no requisitioner asks for more than necessary
   - Buyers can control a requisitioner by asking that notes be taken of the in-process inventory prior to asking for additional stock
   - The EP cost is more vulnerable to attack in the area of in-process inventories
     - Supervision is key

True/False

T F 1. Purchasing processed produce is a simple procedure and does not require many management considerations.

T F 2. Buyers almost exclusively purchase foods processed in ways that enhance the AP price and pay little attention to convenience or taste.

T F 3. All produce can be found in both the frozen or canned state.

T F 4. The EP cost and the AP price are always the same for produce.

T F 5. If a buyer uses bid buying exclusively, he or she may not receive a warning when an AP price shoots up dramatically.

T F 6. If your mother has won a blue ribbon for her home-canned peaches, she is able to sell them to your restaurant as long as they are labeled organic.

T F 7. In some instances, buyers may want to prepare a full recipe with each of the competing bidder's products and then perform their tests.

T F 8. A chef will usually not come to the receiving dock to check the quality of processed products.

T F 9. Dried products should be kept slightly warmer than canned goods to eliminate insects.

T F 10. It is always more advantageous to purchase a Grade C product instead of a Grade B product because of the EP savings.

Fill-in-the-Blank

1. The quality of processed produce and other grocery items are more _____ and the AP prices do not _____ as widely as those for fresh products.

2. The EP cost includes not only the cost of the product but, indirectly, the cost of the _____ it takes to prepare and serve it, the cost of the _____ needed to work with it, and other _____ expenses.

3. When receiving dried processed produce the buyer should check for _____, _____, and _____.

4. Store frozen products at _____ or lower.

5. Organic food is produced without using most conventional _____; fertilizers made with _____ ingredients or _____; _____ or ionizing _____.

6. Canned and bottled products should be stored in a _____ area at approximately _____ °F to _____ °F.

7. _____ can be especially damaging to canned and bottled products.

8. Organic and natural foods tend to be more expensive because there are fewer _____ and the products themselves have a shorter _____.

9. When purchasing canned items, buyers should calculate the _____ also know as _____.

10. The main advantages of pouch packaging over cans, buckets, cartons, and tubs are _____, _____, and _____ convenience.

Multiple Choice

1. Food processing is used for all of the reasons below except:
   a. capturing food items at their peek flavor while adding value to the items
   b. preserving food to increase shelf life
   c. improving flavor of mishandled products
   d. smoothing out seasonal fluctuations

2.   The buyer's selection of a processing method is affected by all but the following:
      a. AP price
      b. convenience
      c. storage costs
      d. consulting services

3.   All of the following are examples of opportunity buys except:
      a. salvage buys
      b. introductory offers
      c. quantity discounts
      d. free delivery offers

4.   Federal grades have been established for all of the following produce and grocery items except:
      a. barbequed
      b. bottled
      c. canned
      d. dried

5.   Grading factors for dried foods include all but the following:
      a. uniformity of size, shape and color
      b. number of blemishes and defects
      c. moisture content
      d. brand name

6.   For Grade A processed foods, buyers expect all but the following:
      a. uniform size
      b. identical taste to fresh product
      c. very best product
      d. excellent color

7.   Generic brands are typically offered at very low AP prices for all but the following reasons:
      a. high pull strategies
      b. often nonexistent advertising costs
      c. lower packaging costs
      d. lower quality (in some cases)

8.   When purchasing large amounts of frozen products, the buyer should address all of the following questions except:
      a. can the package be reclosed tightly
      b. can the packaging be recycled
      c. is the packaging inconvenient for storage
      d. can the packaging be personalized with the company's logo

9.   For the buyer, the advantages of being a house account are all but the following:
      a. receives a higher Brix level
      b. is warned that an AP price may shoot up dramatically
      c. can obtain products that are on shortage
      d. offered low-grade products

10. Buyers' cutting tests include all of the following except:
    a. checking the frozen fruit after it is thawed, especially the texture
    b. thawing and refreezing products to test for color and taste
    c. cooking the frozen vegetables and then test them
    d. reconstitute dried and concentrated products and then test them

Apply Your Knowledge

1. List the standards for your favorite meal using the meat and poultry standards from the USDA (www.ams.usda.gov).

2. Using information from the national organic website (www.ams.gov/nop), explain the difference between 100% organic products and products made with organic ingredients and how you as a buyer can distinguish between the two.

3. One-stop shopping with national corporations has many advantages and disadvantages over local and regional distributors. Review the websites of national corporations such as Sysco (www.sysco.com), Green Giant (www.greengiant.com/), Pillsbury (www.pillsbury.com), and McCormick (www.mccormick.com). Imagine yourself as the new owner of a small 50-room hotel and choose one of these companies that has the ability to provide your new property with all of the products you will need. Explain your answer.

Chapter 19
Dairy Products
After reading this chapter, you should be able to:
- Explain the selection factors for dairy products, including government grades.
- Describe the process of purchasing, receiving, storing and issuing dairy products.

Outline
1. Purchasing dairy products is not easy
   - Numerous varieties and forms of milk, cheeses and frozen dairy foods
   - Butterfat is important, affecting quality including flavor and mouthfeel
     - Amount of butterfat has a direct correlation with the AP price
   - Milk is milk for the most part, but dairies do vary somewhat in quality control programs and processing methods
   - The taste of other dairy products, especially cheese, is unique to the producer
   - Once a buyer settles on a particular brand of cheese, it is difficult to change, especially if the cheese is served alone
   - Buyers almost inevitably become a house account for dairy items such as cheese
   - Items that have substitutes for butterfat can be cost effective
     - Butter vs. margarine
     - Half-and half or non-dairy creamer
     - Natural cheese or cheese food made of vegetable fat
   - Another substitution issue: one dairy item may replace another in recipes
     - Yogurt for sour cream
     - Skim milk for whole milk
     - Pasteurized process cheese for natural cheese
     - These options make it complicated
     - Experimentation is the key
   - Proper representation of substitute products is important, i.e., truth-in-menu legislation
   - With dairy products, a buyer can settle into one-stop shopping or take the time to evaluate the many options
   - All this said, dairy products do not represent a great deal of the purchase dollar but substitution possibilities can be lucrative
2. Selection Factors
   - Management usually determines the varieties and qualities of dairy products to be purchased
     - Intended use
     - Exact name
     - U.S. government grades
       - Agricultural Marketing Service (AMS) of United States Department of Agriculture's (USDA's) Poultry and Dairy Division has set federal grading standards for poultry, eggs and dairy products
       - Grades do not exist for all products
       - Milk is usually graded
         - Grading is voluntary, though many states require federal grading
       - Milk harbors harmful bacteria
         - States have codes covering milk production
         - U.S. Public Health Service's Milk Ordinance and Code (termed the Pasteurized Milk Ordinance or PMO) covers the following
           - Approved care and feeding of dairy cows
           - Handling of milk
           - Pasteurization requirement

113

- - - Holding temperature of milk
  - Dairies have little control over production, but have the option of homogenization or the dividing of the butterfat globules so they stay suspended in the milk
  - Dairies can choose who to sell to: ice cream makers, dry-milk producers, households, etc.
  - Fluid grades are based on bacterial count
    - Grade A – sold in retail stores
    - Manufacturing Grade (Grade B) – used for milk products such as cheese, butter and ice cream
    - Certified grade has very little bacteria and can be used for infants and sick persons (not really a grade but sometimes treated as such)
      - Grader also considers odor, taste and appearance
  - Milk can be fortified with vitamins and other nutrient additives
  - U.S. grading standards have been developed for:
    - Dry nonfat milk: extra; standard
    - Dry whole milk: pemium extra, standard
    - Butter: AA; A; B
  - Wisconsin (as do some other states) imposes grades for cheese and butter
  - Ice cream carries several designations
  - Dating information is important
  - Foodservice buyers usually opt for Grade A milk
  - Because tastes differ from producer to producer government grades are not the main selection criterion for dairy products
- Packers' brands (or equivalent)
- Product size
  - Butter can be ordered in 1-pound prints; 50-pound slabs or chip sizes
- Size of container
  - Important because of perishable nature of product
  - The smaller the unit size the higher the AP price; EP price could be low because of small amount used and less waste
- Type of packaging material
  - Standardized
  - Can select from wide variety of packaging
    - Plastic
    - Fiberboard
    - Metal
    - Glass
    - Aseptic containers
    - Customized also available: cartons with logo; individually wrapped butter chips
- Packaging procedure
  - Example: butter chips layered in a 5-pound container separated by wax paper
  - Example: individually wrapped butter chips
  - Although AP price might be higher for wrapped butter chips, EP might be higher due to packaging that protects shelf-life
- Product yield
  - Buyers should indicate maximum acceptable waste
  - Example: rind on cheese
- Product form

114

- - Example: sliced, grated, whole
- Preservation method
  - Some cheeses don't need refrigeration; buyers should indicate "refrigerated" if they want those cheeses kept at a certain temperature
  - Ice cream is obviously frozen, but some suppliers freeze cheeses and butter; buyers should indicate never-frozen if that is what they want
  - Some items are traditionally canned: evaporated milk, sweetened condensed milk (whole milk can also come this way)
  - Products in aseptic packages can be kept at room temperature for months; pasteurized using "ultra-high temperatures" (UHT); technique is sometimes known as "ultra-pasteurized" (UP)
  - Buyers should specify maximum pull date allowed at time of delivery
- Butterfat content
  - As butterfat goes up, so does the AP
  - High butterfat products are respected: premium ice cream usually contains fresh fruits rather than syrup
  - Buyers should note on spec sheet the degree of "creaminess" they want
- Milk solids content
  - Federal government mandates maximum amount of nonfat dried milk solids allowed
  - Buyers should indicate fewer solids than maximum if that is what they want
- Overrun
  - Definition: amount of air in a frozen dairy product (applies to other dairy products also)
  - Affects flavor
  - Most dairy products are sold by volume – but air is free
  - Federal government standard: one gallon of ice cream must weigh at least 4.5 pounds and contain at least 1.6 pounds of food solids
  - Buyers may be protected on ice cream, but not on whipped topping
- Chemical additives
  - Milk has been kept natural since it is given to babies
  - A few dairy products now contain chemical additives to stabilize, preserve, emulsify product
  - However, dairy products have fewer additives than other processed foods
- Untreated cows
  - Cows are treated with hormones to increase milk production: bST or bovine somatotropin and rBGH or rBST, Recombinant Bovine Growth Hormone
  - Buyers wanting milk from untreated cows should note it on the spec sheet
- How the product is processed
  - Federal standards focus on wholesomeness, not flavor, convenience or packaging
  - Processing may be important depending on the product
    - Cheeses may be aged differently for different lengths of time
  - Buyers may want "natural" processing
- Organic dairy products
  - Demand is growing
- Nondairy products
  - AP prices may be lower
  - Less perishable: save on storage costs; less waste
  - Weight watchers and lactose intolerant guests may want these products
  - Imitations contain chemical additives and don't always have same nutritional value as dairy counterparts
  - Nondairy products may not work in recipes

- AP price
    - Price and credit terms offered by dairies often controlled by local governments (free-market area vs. control state)
    - Few quantity buys available
    - Some items are imported (e.g., cheese); import taxes may apply
- One-stop shopping
    - Buyers can negotiate standing order
    - Dairies deliver often, reducing
3. Purchasing Dairy Products
    - Determining items to purchase and delivery schedule are important because of perishable nature of product
    - Bid buying may be profitable in a noncontrolled state
    - Dairy products comprise small percent of purchase dollars
    - Buyers should evaluate substitution possibilities
    - Distributors carry some dairy products, but a local dairy for fresh milk, some cheeses and ice cream may be best
    - Good to buy locally
4. Receiving Dairy products
    - Examine exterior for dirt, broken containers, faulty wrapping
    - Difficult to confirm that order is complete
        - Number of items in typical delivery
        - Some items usually on standing-order basis; driver will re-stock and give receiver an invoice
        - Supplier substitutions are not always a good match
    - Conduct random taste tests
    - Best to move items to refrigerated area before making inspection
5. Storing Dairy Products
    - Move items to proper area as soon as possible
    - Cheeses
        - Cheeses to be served that day should be left to come to room temperature
        - Cheeses to be served later in the week should be refrigerated; warm temperatures cause cheeses to age, changing appearance, odor and flavor
        - Should stay in original packaging
    - Dairy products pick up odors; should be kept tightly sealed away from odorous foods
    - Products should be rotated on a regular basis
6. Issuing Dairy products
    - Issue older items first
    - Ensure that requisition orders do not request more than is needed to prevent spoilage
7. In-Process Inventories
    - Supervision is the key to prevent spoilage, waste or pilferage

True/False

T F 1.   Butterfat dramatically affects the flavor of a dairy product, but does not impact the AP price as most dairy products are created equal.

T F 2.   There are three federal grades of ice cream: premium, regular and competitive.

T F 3.   Milk has been kept predominately free of additives because it is fed to babies and needs to be pure.

T F 4. Cheese is cheese, aging times and aging methods are not factors the buyer should worry about.

T F 5. Elaborate specifications are required for dairy products because of the number of options available.

T F 6. Homogenization is required by law, pasteurization is left up to the discretion of the dairy.

T F 7. The challenges of purchasing dairy products are compounded by the fact that these purchases represent such a large portion of the annual food expenditures.

T F 8. A buyer should be aware of the fact that prices for dairy products are dramatically different from one dairy to the next.

T F 9. A buyer who simply orders "Swiss cheese" may receive the product sliced, grated or cubed when what he or she really wanted was "whole."

T F 10. Price and credit terms are decided by individual dairies based on fluctuations in demand.

Fill-in-the-Blank

1. _____ and _____ are dairy products that usually come in metal cans.

2. Milk packaged in aseptic containers is considered to be a _____ product because it is pasteurized at _____ or _____ (acronym). This process is also called _____ or _____ (acronym)

3. Cows are sometimes treated with _____, or _____ (acronym) and _____, or _____ (acronym) to increase milk production.

4. _____ is the amount of air in a frozen dairy product (or perhaps in any dairy product). This air content is important in such products as pre-whipped cream in a can and ice cream.

5. Milk with added vitamins A and D or other nutrients is known as _____.

6. _____ is a term for ice cream that contains eggs as a thickening ingredient.

7. The fact that dairy products are so _____ creates challenges in the areas of preservation, packaging, shipping, receiving and storage.

8. The _____ of a dairy product refers to the amount of nonfat dried milk solids it contains.

9. Milk that has an extremely low bacterial count and is given to infants and those who are ill is referred to as _____.

10. An area where the prices and credit terms of dairy products are subject to supply and demand pressures is known as a _____ or _____. The opposite of this is a _____ where prices and credit terms are regulated by the government.

Multiple Choice

1. The standard of identity for milk products is based on which of the following:
   a. butterfat content
   b. degree of fortification with vitamins
   c. pasteurization temperature
   d. amount of nonfat dried milk solids

2. Personal preferences aside, which of the following is not an appropriate pair of substitutions?
   a. yogurt for sour cream
   b. non-dairy creamer for half and half
   c. margarine for butter
   d. all of the examples are appropriate

3. Which of the following is not a grading factor for milk?
   a. appearance
   b. odor
   c. bacterial count
   d. butterfat content

4. What is one reason a buyer might question the wisdom of ordering nondairy products?
   a. they have a longer shelf-life
   b. they often have a lower AP price
   c. the nutritional value is questionable
   d. they provide an option for lactose intolerant guests

5. Which of the following is not a term used to describe the quality of ice cream?
   a. premium
   b. regular
   c. best
   d. French

6. What percent of Americans feel that lowering their exposure to chemicals will result in better health?
   a. 37
   b. 92
   c. 60
   d. 12

7. The Pasteurized Milk Ordinance covers all of the following except:
   a. pasteurization requirements
   b. prices and credit terms offered by dairies
   c. holding temperature of milk
   d. care and feeding of dairy cows

8. Which of the following is not a federal grade for dry nonfat milk?
   a. extra
   b. competitive
   c. standard
   d. all are grades for dry nonfat milk

9.   A buyer must understand the meaning of the term "overrun" for what reason or reasons?
      a. overrun affects the flavor of a frozen dairy product
      b. overrun can affect the volume of a whipped topping
      c. "a" and "b" above
      d. none of the above

10.   Product yield is especially important in relation to:
      a. cheeses with rind
      b. fresh whole milk
      c. condensed milk
      d. ice cream

Apply Your Knowledge
1.   Think about the question of substitutions in relation to dairy products. Imagine that you are a chef at a fine restaurant and the buyer for your company is wanting you to try several substitutes including margarine for butter. Write your "philosophy" about this subject in reply to his request.

2.   If milk contains so few chemical additives, explain the growing demand for organic milk.

Chapter 20
Eggs
After reading this chapter, you should be able to
- Explain the selection factors for egg, including government grades.
- Describe the process of purchasing, receiving, storing, and issuing eggs.

Outline
1. Introduction
   - Purchasing fresh eggs is relatively easy; processed eggs are more of a challenge
2. Selection Factors
   - Intended use
   - Exact name
     o "Fresh shell eggs" refers to eggs that are fewer than 30 days old
     o The term "egg products" refers to eggs that have been removed from their shells for processing
   - U.S. government inspection and grades (or equivalent)
     o Egg Products Inspection Act (EPIA) of 1970 requires the USDA to ensure that egg products are safe, wholesome, unadulterated and accurately labeled
     o Three federal government consumer grades for fresh shell eggs have become familiar quality guidelines
       ▪ U.S. Grade AA
       ▪ U.S. Grade A
       ▪ U.S. Grade B
     o Fresh eggs are graded mainly on interior and exterior quality factors
     o Graders use a process called "candling" to check interior quality of fresh eggs
   - Packer's brands (or equivalent)
     o Buyers do not show a great deal of loyalty for fresh shell eggs
     o Federal grade is the most common quality indicator
     o Packers' brands can be extremely important when purchasing processed and convenience forms of eggs
   - Product size
     o Buyers are normally interested in the size and uniformity of shell eggs
       ▪ Peewee eggs from from younger hens
       ▪ Jumbo eggs come from older hens
     o Buyers usually prefer large-size eggs
   - Size of container
     o For shell eggs, 15-dozen or 30-dozen per case
     o Flat contains 2.5 dozen eggs
     o Processed eggs come in various sizes of containers
   - Types of packaging material
     o Standardized for fresh eggs
       ▪ Snug-fitting fiberboard boxes
     o Improperly packaged products can support bacterial growth
     o Frozen egg products are packaged in moisture-proof, vapor-proof containers
       ▪ Cryovac bags or packaging
       ▪ Metal or plastic containers
     o Dried egg products are generally sold in 6-ounce pouches and 3-pound or 25-pound poly packs
   - Packaging procedure
     o Packaging process not a concern for most egg products

120

- o Buyers may have a specific need for specialized packaging
- Color
  - o Breed of hen determines color of egg
- Product form
- Preservation method
  - o Refrigeration
  - o Oil spraying or dipping
  - o Controlled-atmosphere storage
  - o Procession method
    - ▪ Processed egg product are preserved in a manner other than the shall
- Trust the supplier
  - o More about adequate deliveries and finding a supplier that moves only fresh product
  - o In addition to supplier services buyer must consider purchasing options
    - ▪ Bid buying
    - ▪ House accounts

3. Purchasing Eggs
   - Most widely used quality is U.S. Grade A and the normal size is large
   - Qualities and styles of processed egg products are not easily chosen
     - o Best to consider brand names
     - o No standard of quality for processed egg products
   - Before purchasing egg products, buyers should evaluate substitution possibilities
     - o Bid buying
     - o House accounts

4. Receiving Eggs
   - Examine fresh shell eggs carefully for cracks, dirt, lack of uniformity, and temperature
   - Count eggs or weigh container to make sure all eggs are there
   - The American Egg Board recommends that receivers randomly break a few eggs and inspect them to determine if they meet the guidelines of their given grade
   - Processed eggs usually require other sorts of inspection
     - o Receivers can check frozen egg products for crystallization
     - o Check can pressure of any canned, dried egg products
     - o Check the prices and complete the appropriate accounting procedures

5. Storing Eggs
   - Fresh eggs should be refrigerated as soon as possible at 45°F or below
   - Should be kept in original containers – eggs pick up odors quickly
   - Processed eggs require specific storage environments suggested by the form in which they come
     - o Frozen
     - o Refrigerated
     - o Dry storage

6. Issuing Eggs
   - Properly rotate stock, so that oldest items are issued first (FIFO)
     - o May be accomplished by dating the containers as they are received

7. In-Process Inventories
   - The benefit of good purchasing effectiveness can be offset if the hospitality operators do not control in-process inventories
   - The best a supervisor can do is insist that all eggs be kept in the recommended environment at all times and removed from this environment only when necessary

True/False

T F 1.　A flat contains 18 eggs.

T F 2.　Packaging for fresh eggs is standard.

T f 3.　It is possible to buy pre-cooked plain omelettes.

T F 4.　"Fresh shell eggs" refers to eggs that are less than 45 days old.

T F 5.　There is no nutritional or taste difference between white and brown eggs.

T F 6.　Egg shells are impervious to odors and therefore eggs can be placed anywhere in the refrigerator.

T F 7.　Many suppliers put a protective coating of mineral oil on eggs.

T F 8.　Leaving eggs out all day could cause them to drop a grade.

T F 9.　Peewee eggs are from mature chickens and are also known as runts.

T F 10.　Eggs that have been in controlled atmospheres usually do not go to hospitality operators, they go to the general consumer.

Fill-in-the-Blank

1.　_____ is the term for the process inspectors use to check an egg's interior.

2.　Another word for egg whites is _____.

3.　Eggs that have been removed from their shells for processing are called _____.

4.　_____ is the company that developed vacuum shrink-wrap technology that allows food producers to store foods for great lengths of time. _____ is the name given to this type of packaging.

5.　In addition to quality, buyers are interested in the _____ and _____ of shell eggs.

Multiple Choice

1.　Which of the following determines an egg's color?
　　a. age of the hen
　　b. type of feed given the hens
　　c. breed of the hen
　　d. additives placed in water

2.　Dried eggs are not found in which of the following packaging sizes?
　　a. 6-ounce pouches
　　b. 3-pound poly packs
　　c. 25-pound poly packs
　　d. convenient, single egg, 2-ounce pouches

3. Which of the following grade of eggs is usually purchased by hospitality operation buyers?
    a. Grade AA
    b. Grade A
    c. Grade B
    d. ungraded eggs

4. Which of the temperatures below is the best for storing fresh eggs?
    a. 45°F or below
    b. room temperature
    c. 32° or below
    d. 50° or below

5. Which of the following requires the USDA to ensure egg products are safe?
    a. Egg Inspection Act
    b. Egg Products Inspection Act
    c. Fresh Egg Inspection Act
    d. Fresh Egg Products Inspection Act

Apply Your Knowledge
1. Think about the many convenience egg products mentioned in this chapter. Explain how you might use several of these products in your operation's kitchen and how they might save time and additional ingredient costs.

2. You and the chef are having a discussion about brown versus white eggs. He insists that the additional AP price for brown eggs is justified because brown eggs make a fluffier cake batter and have a more robust egg flavor. What would you do?

Chapter 21
Poultry

After reading this chapter, you should be able to:
- Explain the selection factors for poultry, including government grades.
- Describe the process of purchasing, receiving, storing, and issuing poultry.

Outline
1. Introduction
   - Poultry is a term applied to all domesticated birds used for food
   - Not an especially difficult item to purchase
   - Operations typically buy chicken, turkey, and duckling
   - Major decision: fresh or fresh-frozen
   - Unless the buyers include packers' brands of fresh poultry, the AP price will be about the same among suppliers
   - When buying processed poultry, must decide degree of convenience wanted built into the product
2. Selection Factors
   - Intended use
     - Buyers may want to select poultry items they can use for two or three purposes
     - Fresh poultry should be turned quickly
     - Lower-priced substitutions exist
     - Substitutions can disrupt the production and service functions, however
   - Exact name
     - Federal government has standards of identity for many poultry items
       - Some fresh products are standardized according to the birds' sex and/or age at the time of slaughter
     - Age and sex can affect the intended use of poultry
       - The sex of young birds is not particularly relevant to cooking style
       - In older birds, the differences in taste, texture and yield differ dramatically between the sexes
     - Buyers occasionally encounter defining terminology
       - Free range
       - Kosher
     - Processed products can and will vary significantly among producers
   - U.S. government grades (or equivalent)
     - Poultry inspection became mandatory with the 1957 Poultry Products Inspection Act
     - The Food Safety and Inspection Service of the USDA performs inspections for wholesomeness and federal grading
     - Federal inspectors grade poultry according to several grading factors
       - Conformation
       - Fleshing
       - Fat covering
       - Other factors
     - Several consumer poultry grades exist
       - Grade A
       - Grade B
       - Grade C

- In addition to consumer grades, the federal government offers a "procurement" grading system
  - I
  - II
- Some state and local markets use the following three commercial grades
  - Extra
  - Standard
  - No grade
- A specification for poultry products usually contains some grade reference
- The use of U.S. grades for poultry is very popular in the foodservice industry
  - Buyers usually opt for Grade A products when appearance is important
- Organic
  - Organic requirements: "poultry or edible poultry products must be from animals that have been under continuous organic management beginning no later than the second day of life"
- Packers' brands (or equivalent)
  - For fresh and fresh-frozen poultry, brand loyalty rarely comes into play
  - Some value, as well as higher AP price, is associated with proprietary chicken brand names
  - Brand name items are usually produced in exceptionally clean environments
  - Packers' brands are important to hospitality buyers only when they purchase processed poultry products
- Product size
  - Buyers usually cannot specify an exact product size when purchasing raw poultry products: must indicate the desired weight range
  - General rule: the larger the bird, the higher the edible yield
  - Buyers can normally specify exact size for processed products
- Product yield
  - For some poultry items, buyers may want to indicate maximum yield, or minimum trim
- Size of container
  - Indicate preferred package size
  - Note size of inner packs if applicable
- Type of packaging material
  - Buyers reject packaging that would do anything to shorten a product's shelf life
  - Processed items packaged in moisture-proof, vapor-proof materials that are designed to withstand freezer temperatures
- Packaging procedure
- Product form
  - Virtually endless number of products and forms available
  - Whole birds can be whole or cut into a specified number of pieces
  - Buyers can also opt to have the variety meats included or excluded
  - Cutting and trimming raw poultry adds to the AP price, but enhances convenience
  - Buyers purchasing large amounts of highly processed poultry may indicate formula
- Preservation method
  - Preserved in one of two ways
    - Refrigerated
    - Frozen
  - Operations usually purchase fresh, ice-packed, or chill-packed poultry
  - Some fresh poultry may be preserved with irradiation
    - Irradiation removes almost all traces of harmful bacteria in meat and fish

- Buyers usually purchase processed poultry products in the frozen state
- AP price
  - Raw poultry products offer little spread in AP price from one supplier to another
  - The distance that a finished poultry item must travel to get to a hospitality operation's back door makes a difference
  - AP prices for raw products tend to be more predictable because farmers can produce poultry much more easily and quickly than many other foods
  - AP prices vary quite a bit for processed items
- Trust the supplier
  - AP prices for raw poultry do not vary significantly among suppliers
  - Bid buying not as profitable as with processed products unless additional services are provided

3. Purchasing Poultry
   - Buyers normally use U.S. Grade A quality for poultry
   - Best to prepare a complete specification
   - After preparing the specs, buyers must evaluate potential suppliers
     - The important consideration is supplier services, since quality and AP prices vary only a little

4. Receiving Poultry
   - Conduct customary quality and quantity checks
   - Raw poultry check is not difficult
     - Should be done in refrigerated storage
     - The grade shield is usually displayed on the carton or on the wing of whole birds
     - Receivers must be careful that the boxes have not been repacked
   - Quality check can cause trouble if receivers are concerned with the age of the poultry
     - Receivers can look at the size and amount of abdominal fat
   - Processed products require other types of quality checks
     - Look for proper temperature, signs of thawing and refreezing, and inadequate packaging
     - For canned products, look for leaks, rust, and swollen cans
   - Check quantity
     - Buyers may have to weigh several birds to confirm that they are within the weight range
   - Receiving agents also need to check the types of parts, variety of meats, and processed items
   - Process can be streamlined by using the USDA's Acceptance Service
   - Receivers must check prices and complete appropriate accounting procedures

5. Storing Poultry
   - Hospitality operators should store fresh and frozen poultry immediately at the proper temperatures and humidity
   - Receivers should not handle poultry more than is absolutely necessary
   - Operators might consider keeping a perpetual poultry inventory

6. Issuing Poultry
   - If hospitality operators use a perpetual inventory system, they must deduct the quantity issued
   - Operators should follow proper stock rotation
   - Since these products deteriorate rapidly and are expensive, operators must make sure the requisitioner does not take more than is necessary

7. In-process Inventories
   - The biggest consideration is sanitation

True/False

T F 1. Specifying the intended use for a poultry product is insignificant when ordering these products.

T F 2. Gas-flushed packs are bags with the air completely removed and replaced with carbon monoxide.

T F 3. The first things that must be checked when poultry is received by the hospitality operator are quality and quantity.

T F 4. When ordering whole poultry items, it is difficult or impossible specify size.

T F 5. Selecting a supplier for your poultry needs may result in on-going bidding wars between suppliers.

T F 6. If appearance is important for the poultry product, buyers will most often purchase Grade A quality poultry.

T F 7. The sex of more mature birds is not particularly important to their cooking style or usage.

T F 8. The 1968 Wholesome Poultry Products Act requires state inspection programs to be at least equal to the federal inspection program.

T F 9. Purchasing large birds may be a more economical choice for buyers because they tend to have a higher edible yield.

T F 10. IQF refers to "initially quick frozen."

Fill-in-the-Blank

1. _____ removes almost all traces of harmful bacteria in poultry, meat and fish, and spoilage bacteria in fresh produce.

2. Many refrigerated products are packed at chill pack temperatures. If suppliers do not provide the chill pack alternative, usually they will provide the _____, which gives the same results.

3. The _____ of the USDA performs federal inspections for wholesomeness and federal grading.

4. A bird with some dressing defects, such as a torn skin, or is less attractive because of a visible breastbone would fall under consumer grade _____.

5. Three packer brand labels that buyers can specify when ordering poultry are _____, _____, and _____.

6. For packaging, fresh birds may be slab-packed with crushed ice covering them. This procedure is also known as the _____.

7. The service that streamlines the poultry-receiving process and is popular among large foodservice operators for meat and poultry items, is known as _____.

8.   A bird with a high edible yield is said it have a high _____.

9.   Raw poultry is considered to be a _____, which means for instance that the typical buyer doesn't see a great deal of difference between one frying chicken and another.

10.   _____ poultry must have no preservatives, no artificial ingredients, and must be minimally processed.

Multiple Choice

1.   When selecting poultry products, it is always important to consider the following:
      a. intended use
      b. government grades
      c. exact name of the poultry
      d. all of the above

2.   Chickens that are a little older at slaughter, tend to roam free, and are soaked and salted, are:
      a. free range chickens
      b. salty chickens
      c. kosher chickens
      d. less expensive than other chickens

3.   The poultry inspection law that applies to all raw poultry sold in interstate commerce, as well as to such processed products as canned and frozen items is known as:
      a. Wholesome Poultry Products Act
      b. Poultry Products Inspection Act
      c. State Regulatory Inspection Act
      d. Food Safety Inspection Act

4.   Inspectors, when inspecting poultry, consider several grading factors. They are:
      a. confirmation, fleshing, toning, and other factors
      b. fat covering, form, size of legs, other factors
      c. conformation, fleshing, fat covering, other factors
      d. discoloration, sex, age, type of feathers

5.   Most processed poultry products that the typical hospitality operation purchases are frozen and layered. These items are usually referred to as:
      a. individually quick frozen
      b. gas-flushed pack
      c. cello-packs
      d. ice packed

6.   When purchasing whole birds, buyers often have the option of also purchasing variety meats. Types of variety meats include:
      a. liver
      b. heart
      c. stomach
      d. both a and b

7. Why do AP prices for poultry products tend to be more predictable compared to other products?
   a. because farmers reproduce poultry at a very fast rate
   b. poultry products are difficult to produce
   c. there are more chickens in the world than cows
   d. they are a commodity

8. What is a marinade pack?
   a. packaging that includes different poultry parts
   b. packaging with individual poultry parts soaking in a marinade
   c. packaging that can lengthen the shelf life of poultry
   d. both b and c

9. Poultry, or poultry products from animals that have been under continuous organic management beginning no later than the second day of life are known as:
   a. organic chicken
   b. natural chicken
   c. well-managed chicken
   d. regular chicken

10. Grades that are intended for use by noncommercial, "institutional" food services and are based almost entirely on the amount of edible yield the poultry products contain, are what kind of grades?
    a. federal selection grades
    b. procurement grades
    c. commercial grades
    d. United States Department of Agriculture grades

Apply your knowledge
1. As a buyer, your chef tells you that he/she needs 50 pounds of chicken ordered. Before you can order the chicken, what further information, if any, will you need from your chef?

2. Discuss various ways that you can lengthen the life of poultry once it is delivered to your facility. Why might it be important to be concerned about lengthening the life of your poultry?

3. Congratulations! You are just about ready to open your new restaurant and are finalizing the menu. You have not decided yet whether to serve conventional chicken or perhaps another type of chicken, such as organic or natural chicken. Discuss the details you will need to consider before making your decision about the type of chicken to serve your guests, and why they are important.

Chapter 22
Fish
After reading this chapter, you should be able to:
- Explain the selection factors for fish, including government grades.
- Describe the process of purchasing, receiving, storing and issuing fish.

Outline
1. Introduction
   - Buying fresh fish can be one of the most frustrating jobs in all of purchasing
     - o Few suppliers
     - o Must take what is available
   - Operators can usually get by using processed products
   - Depending on the operation's location, the "fresh" fish may be in tired condition
   - Operators can purchase farm-raised fish
   - Farm-raised fish streamlines fish-purchasing process ensuring consistent quality, supply
   - Fresh fish buyers must be very knowledgeable about fish
2. Selection Factors
   - Intended use
   - Exact name
     - o Many varieties of fish exist in the world today
       - ▪ In the U.S. more than 200 varieties are sold
     - o Buyers must indicate precise name of the item they want
     - o Even if buyer indicates an exact name, could receive an unwanted item because the fish industry is fond of renaming fish
       - ▪ The federal government encourages renaming fish because the public might be more willing to eat certain products if they have more appealing names
       - ▪ Renaming fish is also done as an attempt to increase marketability and profitability
     - o Renaming fish causes problems for the hospitality industry
       - ▪ Receivers must be careful they received what was ordered
     - o Appropriate market terminology is also important
     - o Wise buyers do not rely on standards of identity when preparing specifications for fish products
   - U.S. Government grades (or equivalent)
     - o The U.S. Department of Commerce's National Marine Fisheries Service publishes grade standards and offers grading services for fishery products
     - o The U.S. Government grades few fish items
     - o Grades are based on several factors: appearance, odor, size, uniformity, color, defects, flavor, and texture, as well as point of origin
     - o The federal grades for fish:
       - ▪ Grade A
       - ▪ Grade B
       - ▪ Grade C
     - o When buyers use grade as selection factor, normally U.S. Grade A is specified
   - Packed under federal inspection seal
     - o Fish products not subject to mandatory, continuous federal government inspection
     - o Fish are cold-blooded animals
       - ▪ Diseases affecting them supposedly do not threaten humans who eat them
     - o Fish can be exposed to toxins, bacteria, and parasites harmful to humans

- One way to ensure inspection is to demand all fish products carry a U.S. grade designation
- Only fish produced in the U.S. can carry the federal government's grade or inspection
- The only sure way to obtain fish items that are produced under continuous inspection is to demand that any fish product purchased carry the Packed Under Federal Inspection (PUFI) seal
- Specifying that all fish must carry the PUFI seal will significantly reduce the number of suppliers who can bid for the business
- Packers' brands (or equivalent)
  - Most fresh fish does not carry a brand name
  - Packers' brands for processed fish items abound
  - In some instances, a brand name may be the only guide to seafood consistency
  - Some brand-name, processed fish products carry the U.S. Grade A designation
- Product size
  - Size information is a very important selection factor
  - Shellfish items are usually sized by count and based on 10 pounds
  - Buyers may be able to only specify a weight range for some produces
  - For processed products, buyers may usually indicate the exact desired weight per item
- Product yield
  - Indicate acceptable minimum yield or maximum trim
- Size of container
  - Container sizes vary to satisfy most buyer preferences
  - The size and type of packages available are similar to those available for poultry
- Type of packaging material
  - Fresh fish is usually delivered in reusable plastic tubs or foam containers and packed in crushed ice
  - Processed fish items are usually packaged in cans, bottles, or moisture-proof, vapor-proof materials designed to withstand freezer temperatures
- Packaging procedure
  - Slab-packed, layered, chill-packed, cello packed, and individually quick frozen (IQF)
  - Sometimes available in a marinade pack
  - Fresh shellfish are typically slab-packed
  - Fresh fin fish are normally packed on ice
  - Fresh-frozen fish are usually trimmed, cut, IQF, and packaged on board a fish factory ship
- Product form
  - Fish is processed into many forms
  - Many types of convenience fish products are available
  - Major issues:
    - What are the substitution possibilities?
    - What degree of convenience do you want?
  - Fresh fish may be scarce, but buyers usually have two or more brands of processed fish from which to choose
- Preservation method
  - Fish is preserved in many ways:
    - Frozen
    - Dried
    - Smoked
    - Refrigerated
    - Ice-packed

- Cello packed
- Chill packed
- Live
- Live-in-shell
- Canned
- Packing Medium
  - Water
  - Oil
- Point of origin
  - Influences distinctive character, flavor and texture
  - Advertising point of origin for fish items is a popular practice
  - Substituting items cheats the customer and may violate truth-in-menu legislation
- Trust the supplier
  - When buyers purchase a great deal of fresh fish, they may have to work with one primary supplier
  - Cost-plus purchasing
  - Buyers should deal consistently with trusted suppliers when purchasing fish
  - Processed-fish buying lends itself nicely to bid buying
3. Purchasing Fish
   - Acquire some of the indispensable reference materials available
     - Fish buyers might want to have a copy of the Seafood Handbook
   - Contact FDA Office of Seafood Safety and ask for list of approved interstate fish suppliers operating in the area
   - Decide the exact type of product and quality required and prepare specification
   - If purchasing processed fish in quantity, consider shopping around
   - Before buyers jump at bargains
     - Can employees handle the item properly?
     - Do they have the proper equipment to prepare and serve the new item?
     - If the item is currently on the menu, should menu price be dropped?
     - Should operation use this bargain as a loss leader on the menu?
4. Receiving Fish
   - When a fish shipment is delivered, the receivers' first step is to check its quality
   - Sometimes suppliers will send "slacked-out" fish instead of the product ordered
   - When examining live fish, receivers should see a product that is very active and heavy for its size
   - Live-in-shell crustaceans should also be very active and heavy for their size
     - Live-in-shell mollusk shells should be closed, or at least close when tapped
   - Frozen fish should be frozen solid and packed in moisture-proof, vapor-proof material with no signs of thawing or refreezing and glaze should not be excessive
   - Canned merchandise should show no signs of rust, dents, dirt or swelling
   - Challenge: was the right item received
   - Good quality to one nose may be offensive to another
   - Returning fish may be a problem: the fish may not survive the trip back
   - It can be difficult to judge the quality of frozen or processed items until they are prepared
   - After quality is satisfied, agents should then weigh or count the merchandise
   - If receiving a shipment of shellfish from a supplier on the FDA's Interstate Certified Shellfish Shippers list, a tag in the container will note the number of the bed where the shellfish were grown and harvested
     - If an outbreak of food-borne illness occurs, health officials must be able to determine the lot number of the product so that the remainder can be removed from the channel

- Verify the prices and complete the appropriate accounting documents
5. Storing Fish
   - Fresh fish and fresh, shucked shellfish should be maintained at approximately 32°F and at no less than 65% relative humidity
   - Best stored on a bed of crushed ice and covered with waxed paper to prevent dehydration
     - If crushed ice is not available, store in plastic wrap, aluminum foil, or other suitable container and store in the coldest part of the refrigerator
   - Live fish must be stored in tanks
   - Store frozen fish at or below 0°F; should be stored at −10°F or lower because these temperatures are conducive to maximum shelf life (about three months)
   - Canned or bottled fish should be kept in a dry storeroom with ideal temperature of 50°F, though 70°F is acceptable; storeroom's relative humidity should not exceed 60%
6. Issuing Fish
   - Most fresh fish goes directly into production
   - If fish enters an issue-controlled storage area, issue documents must be prepared when it goes into production
   - Operators should try to avoid the temptation of pre-preparing the fish and then storing portions in the freezer
   - It is absolutely essential for operators to follow proper stock rotation when issuing fish products and that requisitioners do not take more than needed
7. In-Process Inventories
   - A great deal of risk is associated with fish
   - This risk increases dramatically when not handled properly at this step
   - Two rules are paramount
     - Employees should not handle the product needlessly because this spreads bacteria and hastens the deterioration of fish quality
     - Do not pre-prepare any more fish than chefs can use during the shift

True/False

T F 1. Farm raised fish eliminates much of the risk involved in the fish-purchasing process.

T F 2. Fish products can be ordered easily by designating the preferred weight and size.

T F 3. Several imitation fish products, such as imitation shrimp and seafood salad, are made with a fish-based paste called "surama."

T F 4. Americans buy more canned fish than any other type.

T F 5. The USDA monitors imported and interstate fish shipments.

T F 6. Diseases that fish carry can be very dangerous to humans who eat them.

T F 7. PUFI stands for Processed Under Federal Inspection.

T F 8. No federal government policies deal with the sizing system in the fish industry.

T F 9. Live-in-shell items are usually packed in ice or in fresh water.

T F 10. The Seafood Handbook contains twice-weekly market prices for many fish products from various regions of the United States.

Fill-in-the-Blank

1. The _____, the _____, and the _____ are all references that buyers should consult before buying fish.

2. When receivers evaluate live-in-shell mollusks, _____ indicate that the mollusks are fresh.

3. Ordering fish can be complicated. Some companies remove that complication by growing or raising their own fish. _____, as it is called, has been used in China for the past 2,000 years.

4. Fresh fin fish, and shucked shell fish should be stored at approximately _____ (temperature), and _____ percent relative humidity.

5. The U. S. Department of Commerce's (USDC) _____ publishes grade standards for fish products.

6. Grade _____ indicates that the fish is lacking in appearance, has blemishes and is suitable for finished menu items such as soups and casseroles.

7. Processed fish items usually are packaged in _____, _____ or in _____ designed to stand up to freezer temperatures.

8. _____ fish is thawed fish that looks a little dry and has ice spots on it.

9. Major issues that need to bee resolved when purchasing fish are _____ policies and degree of _____ desired.

10. Crab legs and lobster tails are usually sized by count based on 10 pounds. 14/16 crabs legs indicates _____ pieces.

Multiple Choice

1. Fresh fish should be stored:
    a. on a bed of crushed ice covered with wax paper
    b. in water tanks
    c. in dry storage
    d. none of the above

2. A statement of quality, given to the supplier by the buyer, might include:
    a. where the fish is from
    b. the preservation method
    c. the size of the fish
    d. all of the above

3. According to the National Restaurant Association, what type of fish is most commonly farm-raised?
    a. salmon
    b. sea bass
    c. mollusks
    d. catfish

4. Fish naming can vary by locale. For example, "lemon sole" on the East Coast of the United States is a particular size of flounder. In Europe and on the West Coast of the United States it refers to:
    a. flounder
    b. a bigger size of lemon sole
    c. a different type of fish all-together
    d. a shoe

5. The U. S. government only grades a few fish items. An example/s of those items are:
    a. breaded items
    b. pre-cooked items
    c. snails
    d. both a and b

6. HACCP stand for:
    a. Hazard Analysis Critical Control Point
    b. Hazard Analysis Control Critical Point
    c. Hazard Analytical Cost Point
    d. Hazard Analytical Control Point

7. Live-in-shell products are usually packed in:
    a. ice
    b. moisture proof materials
    c. fresh water
    d. none of the above

8. Which of the following substitutions may be considered when purchasing different types of processed fish:
    a. steaks for fillets
    b. headless shrimp for butterfly shrimp
    c. real crab for imitation crab
    d. none of the above

9. Daily prices in fish may fluctuate. Which of the following can a restaurant use to handle those fluctuations?
    a. present those specific items as "specials of the day"
    b. set the menu price based on the fish price, and never change it
    c. hedge the price by buying fish futures
    d. all of the above

10. As opposed to poultry buying, fish buying lends itself nicely to bid buying. What type of fish is typically bought by bidding:
    a. fresh lobster
    b. processed fish
    c. frozen fish
    d. farm-raised catfish

Apply Your Knowledge
1. You have just received a fresh shipment of lobsters from Maine. Discuss why you might note the "point of origin" of the lobster on your menu, and why you might purchase Maine lobster as opposed to other lobster.

2. The delivery person arrives at 5 P.M. with 20 pounds of fresh whitefish. The buyer ordered 20 pounds of fresh snapper. The supplier was out of snapper and sent whitefish. He tried to call earlier, but could not get through. What should the buyer do in this situation?

3. In your own words, discuss the process of receiving fresh fish. What are the challenges that you may face in the process? Why is the entire process important to your restaurant business?

Chapter 23
Meat

After reading this chapter, you should be able to:

- Identify the management considerations surrounding the selection and procurement of meat.
- Explain the selection factors for meat, including government grades.
- Describe the process of purchasing, receiving, storing and issuing meat.

Outline

1. Introduction
   - Meat represents a major portion of the foodservice dollar
2. Types of Meat Items Purchased
   - Foodservice operations purchase some type of beef, veal, pork, or lamb in addition to processed meats
   - Operations use prepared meat entrees to a lesser extent
3. Management Considerations
   - Quality of cuts preferred
   - Should management offer meat on the menu?
   - Alternatives
     - Many alternatives for conventional meat items exist
     - Operators take a chance when they make substitutions
   - The quality desired
     - Quality needs to reflect intended use and image of the establishment
     - Obtaining consistent quality should be a concern when bid buying
   - Type of processing
     - Most buy fresh meat items that are butchered
     - A key factor used in making this decision is the AP price
     - AP price per pound for "portion-cut" meat may differ greatly from the AP price of "wholesale cut" meat
     - In-house meat fabrication presents four major problems:
       - Additional labor hours and skilled laborers
       - Level of pilferage
       - Increased waste
       - Considerable amount of "working" dirt and waste products that must be removed to prevent contamination
     - Disadvantages exist with portion-cut meats
       - A premium may be charged for uniform weight, shape and thickness
       - Pilferage may increase
       - A case of pre-cut steaks may contain one or two steaks of lower quality
     - When purchasing in large quantities, may be advantageous to choose frozen-meat items
     - Another option is convenience foods
   - Reducing the AP price and the EP cost
     - Substitute meat of lower quality and tenderize it
     - Shrink portion sizes
     - Enter into long-term contract with the supplier
     - Hedging may be a way to maintain stable AP price
     - Small operators may have to make do on a day-to-day basis
     - Few meat bargains are available
4. Selection Factors
   - Intended use
   - Exact name

- The federal government has set standards of identity for meat products
- Institutional Meat Purchase Specifications (IMPS) numbering system addresses this issue
  - The IMPS numbers evolved from efforts of the North American Meat Processors Association, the National Live Stock and Meat Board, foodservice purchasing agents, and the USDA's Agriculture Marketing Service Livestock Division
  - Numbers are included in the Meat Buyer's Guide (MBG)
  - The IMPS numbers provide a considerable degree of convenience
- In addition to cuts of meat, buyers need to be knowledgeable about other commonly used trade terms
  - Variety meats
  - Sausages
- U.S. Government inspection and grades (or equivalent)
  - The inspection of meat for wholesomeness made mandatory with the passage of Federal Meat Inspection Act in 1907
  - Inspection falls under the jurisdiction of the USDA's Food Safety and Inspection Service (FSIS)
    - Hazard Analysis Critical Control Point (HACCP)
  - States with companies that sell meats solely through intrastate commerce have the discretion of conducting their own meat-inspection programs
    - State inspection programs are required to be at least equal to the federal inspection programs
  - The inspection of animals is done both before and after slaughtering
  - Meat that passes the rigorous USDA inspection is marked with a federal-inspection stamp
  - In addition to its meat inspection, the USDA offers voluntary grading programs
    - Quality grading systems exist for beef, lamb, pork and veal
    - Grading services are not mandatory but may be purchased
    - Beef are divided into five maturity classes
      - Class A
      - Class B
      - Classes C, D, E
  - The federal quality grades for beef are
    - Prime
    - Choice
    - Select
    - Standard
    - Commercial
    - Utility, Cutter, and Canner
  - The federal quality grades for lamb are
    - Prime
    - Choice
    - Good Utility
  - The federal quality grades for pork are
    - No. 1
    - No. 2
    - No. 3
    - No. 4
    - Utility
  - The federal quality grades for veal are
    - Prime
    - Choice
    - Good

- Standard
- Utility
- Cull
- Product yield
  - The federal government provides a voluntary yield grading service for beef and lamb
    - Yields are numbered 1 through 5
    - Grading factors are based on
      - Thickness of fat over ribeye
      - Area of ribeye
      - Percent of kidney, pelvic, and heart fat
      - Carcass weight
  - If buyers use the IMPS system and/or the USDA yield grades, they can be assured of standardized edible yields for the fresh products they purchase
  - No formal yield grading system is available for pork or veal
- Packers' brands (or equivalent)
  - Many meat producers have developed their own grading procedures
    - Sometimes referred to as "packers' grades"
  - Some producers sell "certified organic" products
    - Qualifying entity must have
      - Standards for what constitutes an agricultural product that is "organically" produced
      - A system for ensuring that the product meets those standards
  - Any type of processed meat, other than fresh-frozen or portion-cut, is often purchased on the strength of a brand name
  - Packers' brands are sometimes used when purchasing portion-cut meats
    - Buyers should be concerned with uniformity
    - Equal weights are not necessarily an indicator of uniform appearance
- Product size
  - Buyers must indicate the size of the particular piece of meat they order
    - MBG notes weight ranges for wholesale cuts of meat; standardized portion sizes for retail cuts
    - Large cuts are categorized into four weight ranges
      - A, B, C, and D
- Size of container
  - Container sizes are standardized in the meat channel of distribution
  - Processed products come in package sizes that normally range from 5 pounds to more than 50 pounds
  - Fresh, portion-cut meat products are usually packed in 10-pound cases
- Type of packaging material
  - Packaging quality has a significant effect on a meat product's AP price
- Packaging procedure
  - The packaging procedure for meat items parallels those procedures used in the poultry and fish channels of distribution
    - Large cuts are usually slab-packed
    - Portion cuts are usually layered
    - Bacon can come in a "shingle pack," a "layout pack," or a "bulk pack"
  - Most suppliers will accommodate buyers' needs if they are willing to pay for these services
- Product form
  - Buyers can use the IMPS numbers when specifying meat cuts

- Preservation method
  - Most meat products are preserved in one of two ways
    - Refrigerated
    - Frozen
  - Canned, dehydrated, and pickled products are also available
  - Meat is also preserved by curing and/or smoking
    - If operators use cured and/or smoked products, buyers must ensure consistent quality by specifying the types of products buyers desire
- Tenderization procedure
  - High-quality meats come with a good measure of natural tenderness
  - The natural tenderization process is referred to as "aging" the meat
    - Dry aging
    - Spraying meat with a mold
    - Wet aging or "Cryovac aging"
  - Another tenderization procedure: "beef electrification"
  - Meat can also be "chemically" or "mechanically" treated to tenderize it
    - Dipping
    - Grinding and cubing
    - Needling
    - Comminuting
- Point of origin
  - Occasionally, a foodservice operator notes on the menu the point of origin for a meat entree
- Inspection
  - Buyers can hire private inspectors to ensure that meat products meet their standards
  - The federal government inspects meat products before they are allowed in the United States
  - This inspection is hampered somewhat because some exporting countries use additives and chemicals that U.S. regulations do not cover
- Imitation meat products
  - Several imitation meat products are available
    - Soybean
    - Oat bran
  - Imitation meat products seem to be very popular in the institutional segment
  - Some foodservice operators like imitation meat products because they can manipulate the fat content
- One-stop shopping opportunity
  - Not every supplier carries all meat products buyers need
- AP price
  - Meat represents a large part of the foodservice purchase dollar
    - AP prices vary for meat items, types of packaging, and any other value-added features
  - The Green Sheet is the trade nickname for the HRI Meat Price Report
  - Buyers might consider quantity buys once or twice a year processed meat items

Purchasing Meat
- First, purchase a copy of the Meat Buyers' Guide (MBG)
- Determine what meat is needed
- Evaluate potential suppliers, determine order sizes, fix order times
- Most meat buyers approach bid buying cautiously
- The quality and style of processed-meat items are not easily decided

- o Packers' brands and suppliers' capabilities weigh heavily in these decisions
  - Buyers should take the time to evaluate substitution possibilities
  - The minimum knowledge the buyer needs can be summarized as follows
    - o Different types of meat
    - o U.S. Grades
    - o Appropriate brand names
    - o Various cuts
    - o Intended use
8. Receiving Meat
   - Many owner-managers insist inspections be done in the walk-in refrigerator
   - The chef, or someone knowledgeable, should handle quality check
   - Receiver must be able to determine that what the buyer ordered matches what is being received
   - The receiver should check the condition of the meat
     - o Color
     - o Odor
     - o Slimy appearance
     - o Packaging
     - o Temperature
   - The receiver should also check quantities
     - o Weight, count, and sizes
   - After quality and quantity checks, the receiver should check prices
   - Controlling meat purchases requires a strong emphasis on record keeping
     - o Receiving sheets, bin cards, and meat tags
   - Hospitality operators can streamline the meat-receiving process by using the USDA's Acceptance Service
   - A related USDA program is the "Product Examination Service"
9. Storing Meat
   - Whether fresh or frozen, meat must be kept clean and cold
   - Stock must be rotated properly
   - Meat products are susceptible to bacterial contamination
   - Store fresh meat in a meat refrigerator apart from cooked meat items at a temperature of 35°F to 40°F
   - To avoid contamination from raw-meat droppings, operators should place cooked items above raw meats
   - Operators should not wrap fresh meat too tightly or stack it too tightly
   - Store frozen products at -10°F or lower
10. Issuing Meat
    - Operators should properly rotate stock so that the oldest items are issued first
    - Meat is rarely received and sent straight to production
      - o An employee typically needs a stock requisition to get it
      - o Requisitioner should return any unused meat at the end of the work shift
      - o The meat consumed should be consistent with the guest check
11. In-Process Inventories
    - In-process meats cause relatively little trouble
    - The penalties for pilferage and waste are normally quite severe
    - Operators can reduce the number of "errors" by demanding that mistakes, along with the rest of leftover meat, be turned in at the end of the shift
    - Effective supervision is the best answer

True/False

T F 1. Meat usually accounts for the largest portion of the foodservice purchase dollar.

T F 2. The AP price of meat may be reduced by purchasing lower quality meat.

T F 3. All meat products, including rabbit, must be inspected by the federal government.

T F 4. The federal government provides 5 levels for yield grading.

T F 5. Most meat is packed using the ice pack method.

T F 6. Meat can be dry-aged by spraying it with mold.

T F 7. MBG stands for Manager's Buyers Guide

T F 8. One challenge to buying quality meat relates to bid buying.

T F 9. Fresh meat comes in two basic cuts.

T F 10. The federal inspection of meat is done once the meat is delivered to the hospitality operator.

Fill-in-the-Blank

1. In addition to the various cuts of meat, _____ and _____ are two other commonly used trade terms.

2. The _____ of 1907 made the inspection of meat mandatory.

3. EP cost refers to _____.

4. Yield Grade _____ represents the highest yield of cuts for beef.

5. Beef animals are categorized into _____ maturity classes.

6. IMPS stands for _____.

7. MBG stands for _____

8. The federal quality grades for lamb are _____, _____, _____, _____.

9. Other than refrigerated or frozen, two other types of meat preservation are _____ and _____.

10. Tenderizing meat using a flaking and reforming process is known as _____.

Multiple Choice

1. This type of aging involves wrapping the meat cuts in heavy plastic vacuum packs, sealing them tightly, and keeping them refrigerated for about 10 to 14 days:
   a. wet aging
   b. ziploc aging
   c. dry aging
   d. natural aging

2. Bacon is packed in what way?
   a. shingle pack
   b. layer pack
   c. bulk pack
   d. all of the above

3. High quality veal is based on:
   a. its red color
   b. its rough flesh
   c. its pink color
   d. how much bone there is

4. Meat that is very tender and juicy, with 8 to 10 percent fat, is what grade of beef?
   a. Prime
   b. Choice
   c. Standard
   d. Select

5. FSIS stands for:
   a. Federal Safety and Inspection Service
   b. Food Safety and Inspection Service
   c. Food Service and Inspection for Safety
   d. Food Standards and Inspection Service

6. Variety meats may include items such as:
   a. liver
   b. heart
   c. ears
   d. both "a" and "b"

7. The numbers that managers can use when ordering meat are known as:
   a. IMPS numbers
   b. NAMP numbers
   c. MBG numbers
   d. all of the above

8. Factors that meat graders consider when grading meat include all of the following except:
   a. age at time of slaughter
   b. the color of the flesh
   c. the color of the fur
   d. the shape and form of the carcass

9. Fat streaking in the ribs and the fat streaking in the inside flank muscles of lamb is called:
   a. streaking
   b. marbling
   c. feathering
   d. too much fat

10. Fresh meat can spoil quickly, therefore fresh meat should immediately be stored in a cooler between:
    a. 0°F and -10°F
    b. 0°F and 10°F
    c. 10°F and 30°F
    d. 35°F and 40°F

Apply Your Knowledge

1. Your restaurant has typically served only chicken and fish as main entrees. You have noticed, however, the increasing popularity of steakhouses and have now decided to serve steak in your restaurant. Discuss the type and quality of meat you will select, how it will be aged and tenderized and its intended use. Where and how will you purchase it? Provide the specification for your order

2. You have recently hired a new buyer for your meat products. Since that buyer's arrival, you have noticed that the types and grades of meat that are delivered are not what you normally use and your customers expect. Discuss what you think the problem may be, and how you will fix it.

3. Meat can be tenderized in many ways. As the owner of the most popular steakhouse in town, share with your guests the process that you use. Also explain how you decided on that process versus other tenderizing techniques. What are the advantages of your technique over other techniques?

Chapter 24
Beverages
After reading this chapter, you should be able to:
- Identify management considerations surrounding the selection and procurement of beverage alcohols and nonalcoholic beverages.
- Explain the selection factors for beverage alcohols and nonalcoholic beverages
- Describe the process of purchasing, receiving, storing and issuing beverage alcohols and nonalcoholic beverages.

Outline
1. Introduction
   - Beverage alcohols include wines, beers, and spirits
   - Beverage alcohol products are easiest items a buyer can purchase
     - Standardized products manufactured under controlled conditions
     - The quality of beverage alcohol is very consistent
   - Many customers tend to order a preferred, or "call" brand
   - Some suppliers are exclusive distributors for one or more products in an area
   - State governments sometimes regulate and control the manufacturing, possession, sales, transportation, and delivery of beverage alcohols
     - Buyers must follow specific ordering and bill-paying procedures
   - Some states regulate beverage alcohol commerce through "licenses"
   - License states are allowed to offer credit terms, while in control states, buyers must pay cash for an order
2. Management Considerations
   - Problems associated with beverage alcohols rarely center on purchasing procedures
     - Should we offer beverage alcohol service to guests?
       - Many foodservice operations profit from food and beverage alcohol sales
         - Food sales are generally less profitable
         - Beverage sales easier to produce
         - Hospitality operators must note decline in U.S. liquor consumption
         - Basis for decline may be attributed to
           - Increased health and nutrition concerns
           - Laws prohibiting happy hours
           - Tougher DWI and DUI laws
           - Social pressures created by groups such as MADD
       - Different states have different "Dram Shop" laws
         - Rules as to who can be held liable for an alcohol-related accident
       - Operations must obtain liquor license or permit
       - Other expenses
         - Increased liability insurance premiums
         - License renewal costs
         - Government-mandated record-keeping requirements
         - Participation in safe-driver or designated driver programs
         - Employment of floorperson or bouncer to restrict minors
       - Some operations try maintain profit margins by capitalizing on consumer trend toward drinking more wine, beer and nonalcoholic beverages
     - What quality of beverage alcohol should we serve?
       - The value of premium brands versus nonpremium brands
       - Generally, AP price difference at wholesale between a call brand and well brand is not too significant

- Another difference between comparable liquor brands is the "proof"
- o Should we serve draft beer, bottled beer or both?
  - Many guests prefer draft beer
    - o Draft beer is difficult to serve properly
  - Acquiring the preferred draft beer brands may not be possible
- o Which wines should we serve?
  - Buying wines is trickier than buying other beverage alcohols
  - Buyer needs considerable product knowledge
  - Choices must complement the customers' dining experience
  - Major concern: how many varieties and types of wines to carry
    - o Operational challenges
      - Wine is difficult to store properly
      - Requires considerable storage space
      - May be in storage for a long time before it sells
      - Personnel must be trained to sell and serve correctly
      - A variety of wines may require a variety of suppliers
  - A substantial wine inventory can mean tying up large amounts of capital
  - A well-stocked wine cellar can offer many advantages
    - o Prestige
    - o Indulging and pleasing patrons
    - o Marketing edge
    - o Bigger profits
- o The appropriate number of brands of distilled spirits and beer to carry
  - Few patrons expect a wide choice of beers
  - Guests can be annoyed when call brand is not available
  - Deciding what to carry is not easy
- o The appropriate menu price for beverage alcohols
  - Customers are sensitive to menu prices for beverage alcohols
    - o Must emphasize service and other value-added features
  - Many customers are switching to wine, beer and nonalcoholic beverages
  - An operation must achieve a certain profit margin per drink
3. Selection Factors
   - Intended use
   - Exact name
     - o Numerous types and variations of beverage alcohols exist
     - o Buyers must specify the exact name of the item
     - o Standards of identity exist for many items
   - Brand name (or equivalent)
     - o The most fundamental selection factor is brand name
       - Tends to be the only characteristic a patron considers
     - o Where law allows, customized brand labels may be available
       - Private labeling of wines is common
       - Enhances the hotel's advertising and promotion program
   - Vintage
     - o The year in which the wine is produced
       - Associated with most fine wines
       - Essential selection criterion
     - o Skilled buyers also consider the wine manufacturer
   - Alcohol content
     - o Beverage alcohols have varying levels of alcohol content

- State or local government controls the alcohol content of these beverages
- Due to different proofs, buyers must avoid ordering unusable products
- Size of container
  - Package sizes are standard
  - Buyers must determine size that best fits needs
- Type of container
  - Packaging materials are also standardized in the beverage alcohol distribution channel
    - Cases
    - Kegs
    - Plastic or glass bottles
    - "Bag-in-the-box" packages
  - Some opportunities to personalize beverage containers
    - Impressive merchandising effect and customer experience
  - Some suppliers also number or code the liquor containers
    - Provides a means of inventory control
- Point of origin
  - Very important selection factor for wines
  - Implies taste variations
- Preservation methods
  - Wines and canned and bottled beers should be maintained at cool temperatures
    - Draft beer, with the shortest shelf life of all, should be refrigerated
  - Store wines and beers in a dark environment
    - Light has a negative impact on these products
- AP Price
  - Normally, buyers must pay the going price for liquor items
  - Quantity buys for beverage alcohols are available
  - Another way to save is by purchasing the largest possible containers
  - States sometimes permit distributors to offer price discounts
    - "Post-offs"
  - Buyers must also be concerned with import duty
    - Taxes and tariffs levied on imported products impact AP price
- Supplier services
  - For well brands, management has a choice about which brands to use
  - Supplier services include
    - Simplification of clerical routines
    - Classes in understanding and complying with local liquor codes
    - Reasonable minimum-order requirements
  - The law severely restricts what suppliers can do for their customers
4. Purchasing Beverage Alcohols
- The liquor industry provides information on products, distributors, and AP prices
- Biggest decision is how much to order
  - Typical par stock is set for one week
- "Broken case"
- Buyers face two other major decision points when purchasing beverage alcohols
  - Post off opportunity
  - The need to purchase a very large supply of one brand
- Specifications are important
- It is possible for buyers to contract a winery, brewery, or distiller to prepare products according to special formulas

5. Receiving Beverage Alcohols
   - Receiver is generally a supervisor, owner-manager, or an assistant manager
   - Hospitality firms may employ a sommelier, or wine steward
     - This expert does it all: buys, receives, stores, and sells wine in the dining room
   - Receiver checks quantities and compares invoices against POs and beverage labels
   - Beer kegs can present some receiving difficulty
   - Receiver must compute amount of required deposits for bottles and kegs and ensure the company receives credit for them when returned to the distributor
   - Receiver must complete government-required paperwork
6. Storing Beverage Alcohols
   - Storing beverage alcohol is easier than storing many other food products
   - Stolen liquor can be easily converted into cash
     - Store in a well-secured, locked facility with as few individuals given
     - Many operators maintain a perpetual inventory of beverage alcohols
   - Distilled spirits, wine, and beer all have unique storage requirements
     - Distilled spirits
       - Requires little care, and storage life is long
       - Store in a dry area devoid of direct sunlight and excessive heat
     - Wine
       - Wines are harder to store than other beverage alcohols
       - Require specific temperatures and humidity conditions
         - Red - cool area
         - White - refrigerated
         - Cork-bottled wines are stored on their side
         - Screw-top and fortified wines can be stored upright
         - Kept away from excessive heat or widely fluctuating temperatures
       - Some wines improve in flavor as they age in the bottle
       - Wine sold in "bag-in-the-box" or other bulk containers ("jug wine") is often used as house wine
       - Use a wine dispensing unit or reseal the bottle tightly and refrigerate to store opened bottles of wine sold by the glass or leftover wine
       - Leftover wine may be used for cooking
     - Beer
       - Keg beer is not pasteurized
         - Refrigerate at approximately 36°F to 38°F
         - Should not keep kegs more than two weeks
         - Store beer kegs in walk-in refrigerator that is close to the bar
       - Most canned and bottled beer is pasteurized
         - Canned beer has a shelf life of approximately four months if refrigerated
         - Bottled beer has a shelf life of approximately six months
         - Once a can or bottle is opened, there is no way to save leftovers for later
7. Issuing Beverage Alcohols
   - Employees rarely have the authority to get their own beverage alcohols
     - A receiver prepares a stock requisition
     - Possible requirement: turn in an empty bottle for every full one requested
     - Set strict par stocks for beverage alcohols
   - In banquet or temporary bars, the assistant manager or head bartender will stock the bar to bring up to par; additional stock obtained from the head bartender or assistant manager
     - At the end of the shift, all remaining stock is returned or locked in a liquor station
     - Head bartender or assistant manager counts what is left and determines the liquor usage

- o The quantity of liquor is converted to theoretical sales and should agree with sales recorded on the cash register and the amount of cash or drink tickets collected
- Before issuing beverage alcohols management may want to code the bottles with a number or some other mark that can only be seen with an infrared light
- Operations with an automatic bar system can simplify the issuing process

8. In-Process Inventories
   - The primary concern with beverage alcohol is personnel control
     - o The most effective tool is employee supervision

9. Nonalcoholic Beverages
   - Management considerations
     - o Number of varieties to carry
     - o Soft drinks in bottles and cans or use dispensing machines
     - o Finding the right coffee supplier
   - Selection factors
     - o Intended use
     - o Exact name
       - ▪ Some nonalcoholic beverages have standards of identity, while some do not
     - o U.S. Government grades (or equivalent)
       - ▪ Grades exist for
         - o Juices
         - o Green tea
         - o Milk
     - o Brand name (or Equivalent)
       - ▪ Brand names are important for buyers
       - ▪ Must remain mindful of copyright laws and proprietary rights of suppliers
     - o Size of container
       - ▪ 6-ounce, single serve to 5-gallon kegs
     - o Type of container
       - ▪ Different sizes and types of containers available
       - ▪ Personalized packaging may be available
     - o Product Form.
       - ▪ Can purchase ready-to-serve beverages
       - ▪ With postmix products, buyers save a few dollars by adding own labor
       - ▪ Buyers can purchase most nonalcoholic beverages in varying degrees of form value: the more convenient the form, the higher the AP price
     - o Preservation method
       - ▪ Generally, suppliers deliver premix products at room temperature
       - ▪ Depending on the type of item, postmix products are held under refrigerated, freezer, or dry storage temperatures
     - o AP price
       - ▪ Higher quality implies higher AP price
       - ▪ EP cost can also rise disproportionately for some nonalcoholic beverages
       - ▪ Some states require wholesale price maintenance for some nonalcoholic beverages
     - o Supplier services
       - ▪ Supplier services are crucial when buyers purchase nonalcoholic beverages
       - ▪ With two similar brands to choose from, buyers will select the one that carries more supplier services
       - ▪ "Equipment programs"

- Delivery schedules, ordering procedures, and minimum-order requirements are important
10. Purchasing Nonalcoholic Beverages
    - Purchasing procedure follows a routine program
    - Order and delivery schedules are pretty well set
    - Buyer's primary decision is how much to order
    - Some suppliers stipulate minimum-order requirements
    - Opportunity buys are infrequent
11. Receiving Nonalcoholic Beverages
    - Use suggested receiving principles noted in chapter 14
    - Receivers check the quantity, AP prices, and condition of the delivered goods
    - Correctly account for any returned merchandise to ensure proper credit is received
12. Storing Nonalcoholic Beverages
13. Issuing Nonalcoholic Beverages
    - Managers and owners slight nonalcoholic beverage control for three major reasons
        o Cost of controlling can be higher than potential savings
        o Employers may permit employees to drink some beverages for free or for a small "drink fee"
        o Beverages may get shifted back and forth between the bar, the kitchen, room service, and poolside service, which makes monitoring difficult
14. In-Process Inventories
    - Many problems with nonalcoholic beverages center on the pre-preparation, preparation, and service functions
    - Supervision is key

True/False

T F 1. Alcohol that is 70 proof is the highest proof alcohol that can be purchased.

T F 2. Wines that are packed in a plastic liner and then placed into a cardboard box have "bag-in-the-box" packaging.

T F 3. It is legal to serve alcohol to people under the age of 21.

T F 4. Beer should be stored in a freezer to preserve its quality.

T F 5. A major challenge for receiving and storing alcohol is pilferage.

T F 6. The EP cost per serving is sometimes known as the "drink cost."

T F 7. When deciding to serve non-alcoholic beverages, management must consider the variety of products to serve.

T F 8. "Juice" on a label or package implies that 50% of the product is derived from the fruit or vegetable.

T F 9. When purchasing non-alcoholic beverages, buyers place a strong emphasis on supplier services.

T F 10. Keg beer should be refrigerated at approximately 36°F to 38°F.

Fill-in-the-Blank

1. _____ is an indication of alcohol strength.

2. Beverage alcohols such as wine, beer, and spirits are also known as _____.

3. Many customers have a favorite brand of alcohol they order when in a bar or restaurant known as a _____ brand.

4. A beverage product that is 100 percent derived from a fruit or vegetable, with no water added is called _____.

5. Beverages that can be purchased in bottles, plastic cartons, waxed cartons, cans, kegs, and bag-in-the-box containers and are ready-to-serve are called _____ beverages.

6. If a restaurant manager wishes to save a bottle of open wine, or serve wine by the glass, a process known as _____ may be used to eliminate the oxygen from the bottle. This will help maintain a proper storage environment.

7. Rum that is 100 proof has _____ percent alcohol.

8. DWI stands for _____.

9. _____ states are those where the state or local government stipulates that beverage alcohols must be sold at minimum wholesale prices and minimum retail prices.

10. Laws that basically provide rules as to who can be held liable for an alcohol-related accident are called _____ laws.

Multiple Choice

1. Wine is a popular item on menus today. It does, however, provide operational challenges to management. Those challenges include all of the following except:
   a. wine can be difficult to store
   b. wine requires a lot of room to be stored
   c. personnel must be trained to sell and serve it properly
   d. the capital costs for wine inventory can be quite low

2. House wines are sometimes known as jug wine or:
   a. cheap wine
   b. bag-in-the-box wine
   c. wine served in a decanter
   d. bottle wine

3. Suppliers will sometimes lend, for example, the use of brewing equipment, dispensing equipment, coffee pots and so forth to hospitality operations, in exchange for the purchase of beverage products. This type of arrangement is referred to as:
   a. a convenience arrangement
   b. a free coffee arrangement
   c. an equipment program
   d. a minimum order requirements

4. Cork wine should be stored on it side because:
    a. it keeps the cork moist
    b. more wine can fit into a wine cellar if the bottles are on their side
    c. it enables air to get to the wine
    d. none of the above

5. The beverage produced by the fermentation of grains after the starch in them is converted to sugar is called:
    a. whiskey
    b. bourbon
    c. moonshine
    d. beer

6. In some states the state government controls the manufacturing, possession, sale, transportation, and delivery of beverage alcohols. These states are known as:
    a. government states
    b. control states
    c. license states
    d. dictator states

7. DUI stands for
    a. driving under intoxication
    b. driving under the influence
    c. drinking under the influence
    d. drinking under intoxication

8. Non-alcoholic products, usually in concentrate form, that require someone on the staff of the hospitality operation to do some additional preparation are called:
    a. postmix products
    b. remix products
    c. orange juice
    d. frozen products

9. The purpose of Dram Shop laws is to:
    a. stop people from drinking and driving
    b. encourage people to use a designated driver
    c. provide rules as to who can be held liable for an alcohol-related accident
    d. sue people when they drink and drive

10. All wines should be stored at cool temperatures in order to maintain their quality. Different wines are served, however, at different temperatures. White wine is traditionally served at what temperature?
    a. about 39°F
    b. about 41°F
    c. about 42°F
    d. about 40°F

Apply Your Knowledge
1. Assume that you own a small neighborhood tavern. You employ one bartender and one assistant manager that help with the entire operation. The assistant manager also tends bar. Who should order the alcohol items? Why? Who should receive and store them? Why?

2. That state in which you have your bar has the Dram Shop Law. In essence, you will be held liable if someone you serve alcohol to leaves your establishment and causes an accident. What should you do, as the bar owner, to limit your liability? What service might you offer your customers to discourage them from drinking and driving? How do you deal with customers who have already had too much?

3. You have just opened a new bar in town. You have decided to serve premium well brands. Explain your rationale for this choice and its advantages and disadvantages.

Chapter 25
Nonfood Expense Items

After reading this chapter, you should be able to:

- Identify management considerations surrounding the selection and procurement of nonfood expense items.
- List the types of nonfood expense items that might be purchased by a hospitality operator.
- Describe the major selection factors for nonfood expense items.

Outline

1. Introduction
   - Some operations devote a great amount of money to nonfood expense items
     - Referred to as "operating supplies"
     - Not a capital item
   - Buying nonfood items is sometimes a highly routine activity
     - Department heads responsible for ensuring an orderly flow
   - Small operations tend to view these purchases as nuisances
2. Management Considerations
   - Personalization of nonfood Items
     - The degree of personalization is related to the image the operation wishes to create
     - When buyers purchase personalized items, they have to divide it into two components:
       - Advertising
       - Functional
     - Image is crucial to the sale of nonfood items
     - Should serve operation's needs for a long time
   - Nonfood product variety
     - Many products and suppliers
     - Favors bid buying
   - Degree of product convenience
     - Form economic value comes into play with nonfood items
       - Greater convenience, greater form value, higher AP price
     - Disposable versus reusable
   - Nonfood impulse purchasing
   - Supervising nonfood items
     - Supervisors should strictly monitor the usage of nonfood items
     - Frequent stockouts can occur
   - Quantity and volume discounts
   - Nonfood packers' brands
     - Packers' brands as a selection factor not as prevalent with nonfood items
   - Systems sale
     - Occurs when buyers purchase a particular product that can accept supplies (e.g., guest checks or cash register tapes) from only one company
     - Consider trade-off when offered a systems sale
   - Operating-supplies schemes
     - Hospitality operations are more vulnerable to rip-off artists in the nonfood expense items, capital equipment, and service channel
     - Salespersons may offer what appears to be tremendous bargains, but the merchandise delivered is often inadequate
     - Follow rigorous selection and procurement procedures for all products and services
   - Safety considerations
     - Some nonfood items may present a safety hazard

- o Store and use such items properly
- o Hire someone to perform the tasks associated with toxic products
- New versus used
  - o Can purchase some items in used condition
  - o Must be willing to take chances and spend time and effort to locate the merchandise
- Equipment program
  - o Equipment programs are available for some nonfood items
  - o Similar to those for nonalcoholic beverages
  - o Eliminates the need to invest in equipment and maintenance
- Lifetime cost
  - o Some nonfood expense items have a long life
  - o Buyers must consider
    - Original AP price
    - Operating costs
    - Potential salvage value
- Credit terms
3. Purchasing Nonfood Expense Items
   - Can purchase nonfood items several ways
   - Major problem is identifying the proper par stock and appropriate supplier
   - Multiunit operations save the most when exercising quantity buying power
   - Franchisees tend to purchase from the company commissary
   - First step is to determine exactly what is required
   - Good idea to prepare specifications for each item
4. Typical Nonfood Items that Hospitality Operators Use
   - Cleaning Supplies
     - o Examples: guest supplies; chemical cleaners; soaps; detergent; bleach
     - o Selected on the basis of the following factors:
       - As-used cost
       - Product effectiveness
       - Adaptability
       - Product safety
       - Ease of use
       - Odor
       - Container size
       - Supplier services
     - o Storage of cleaning supplies can present some difficulty
     - o Must store away from foods and beverages to avoid contamination
   - Cleaning tools
     - o Mops, buckets, vacuum cleaners, pot brushes and squeegees
     - o Factors affecting purchase decisions
       - Cost
       - Employee skill
       - Material used to make the item
       - Used tools
     - o In-process storage and use can create problems
       - Keeping tools maintained can be difficult
   - Maintenance supplies
     - o Includes light bulbs, plumbing parts, and other similar items
     - o Selection factors
       - Cost

- Labor availability
- Used supplies
- Sizes
- Capitalizing expenses
  - Two unique issues
    - Should carry a lot of these supplies in stock
    - Maintenance schedules can troublesome
- Permanent ware
  - Initial investment in permanent ware may be a capital expenditure
  - After initial delivery, replacements are considered a cost of doing business
  - Examples: plates; silver; glasses; ashtrays
  - May have the option of using disposables for some or all of these
  - Selection factors include
    - Permanent ware needed
    - AP price
    - The need to match
    - Source of supply
    - Material used to make the item
    - Sizes
    - Length of service
    - Used permanent ware
  - Difficulties can occur with the in-process inventory
  - Operators may be tempted to replace the original item with a cheaper imitation
- Single-service disposable ware
  - Some states and local municipalities restrict the use of disposable ware
  - Several types of disposable ware are available from a multitude of suppliers
  - Selection factors include
    - What do you need?
    - Packaging
  - Waste can become a problem if operators let customers help themselves or permit employees to use the items indiscriminately
- Preparation and service utensils
  - Initial investment may be treated as a capital investment
  - Replacement items treated as a current expense
  - Selection factors noted for permanent ware are the same as those for preparation and service utensils
  - Using disposable products is an option
  - Operators must closely supervise the in-process usage of these items
- Fabrics
  - May need to acquire several types of fabrics
    - Buy them
    - Lease them
    - Use disposables
  - Operations can buy and clean uniforms or leave this up to the employee
  - Additional considerations:
    - Length of service
    - Maintenance
    - Who chooses
    - Fabric types
  - Receiving and storage are not particularly difficult

- - In-process care and maintenance can cause challenges
  - Other paper products
    - Examples: guest checks; cash register tapes; tissues; doilies
    - Selected according to the following factors
      - Image
      - Special requirements
      - Personalization
      - AP Price
      - Minimum-order requirements
    - Purchasing, receiving, and storing these products rarely present problems
    - In-process inventory may generate some waste
  - Miscellaneous Items
    - Products such as pest control and plant food fall into this category
    - Avoid purchasing many of these items and avoid storing them on premises
    - These materials could contaminate food and injure guests and employees
    - Same selection factors apply

True/False

T F 1. Image is not important in the selection of most nonfood items.

T F 2. Nonfood items may often become advertising tools for operators.

T F 3. Bid buying may be very beneficial when purchasing standard nonfood items such as plain napkins and ordinary flatware.

T F 4. Purchasing large amounts of nonfood items at one time is a great way to take advantage of possible volume discounts.

T F 5. Estimating life-time cost involves the original AP price as well as operating costs associated with the use of the product.

T F 6. The most important step in buying nonfood items is for buyers to determine exactly what they want.

T F 7. The in-process inventory for permanent ware is fairly easy to track.

T F 8. Buyers may buy disposable uniforms, costumes, hat, and shirts.

T F 9. Personalization of paper products, or other non-food items, tends to be less expensive that non-personalized items.

T F 10. One problem associated with non-food items is the difficulty in supervising the employees when they use them.

Fill-in-the-Blank

1. There are many suppliers of nonfood items, and many nonfood items from which to choose. This situation favors _____ buyers.

2. _____ provides safety regulations for storage and use of toxic chemicals such as cleaning products, paint, or other similar products, that, when handled incorrectly, may impose health hazards.

3. Purchasing nonfood items can be challenging. Two major problems with purchasing nonfood items are determining the _____ and the _____.

4. Purchasing a product but arranging to store it with the supplier is known as a _____.

5. Hospitality operators purchase nonfood items for nine categories. Four of those categories include _____, _____, _____, and _____.

6. Adaptability and product safety are two areas of concern that are associated with purchasing _____ supplies.

7. Purchasing major equipment often involves the manager or owner of a company. When these purchases are made, their expenses, rather than being normal expenses, are _____ expenses.

8. When purchasing personalized products such as paper napkins, large quantities are usually ordered. Oftentimes, the supplier may even have a _____ requirement.

9. _____ is the length of time a particular item will be used. Buyers use this to help them decide what the quality of the product should be; for example, higher quality for longer use.

10. The purchase of nonfood items may come with free equipment use. This type of arrangement is known as an _____.

Multiple Choice
1. Which of the following presents a challenge for purchasing cleaning tools:
   a. receiving the tools
   b. storing the tools
   c. there are no challenges
   d. maintaining the tools

2. To help save the environment, buyers can do what when making their purchases?
   a. only buy Styrofoam products
   b. buy products with minimal packaging
   c. buy in bulk
   d. both "b" and "c"

3. When choosing fabric, the following must be considered:
   a. length of service
   b. product safety
   c. personalization
   d. packaging

4. What type of operations save the most when they exercise their buying power?
   a. independent operations
   b. mom and pop operations
   c. multi-unit operators
   d. all operations

5. Similar to purchasing liquor, buyers of nonfood items tend not to use
   a. specifications
   b. wholesalers
   c. discounts
   d. a salesperson

6. When purchasing maintenance suppliers, buyers analyze:
   a. who will be doing the labor and how long it will take
   b. should new or used maintenance equipment be purchased
   c. what the cost will be
   d. all of the above

7. Disadvantages to buying used nonfood items include all of the following except:
   a. the buyer must take time to find the product
   b. it is expensive
   c. the quality may not be as good as new
   d. delivery must be arranged by the buyer

8. When computing as-used cost of a lifetime product, it is important to consider:
   a. the product's original AP price
   b. how big the product is
   c. the operating costs of the product
   d. both "a" and "c"

9. Operating supplies are also referred to as:
   a. supplies we don't operate
   b. supplies we don't always use
   c. nonfood expense items
   d. expense items

10. What kind of item is one that can be written off in the current year's income statement?
   a. capital item
   b. current item
   c. expense item
   d. food and beverage item

Apply Your Knowledge

1. The concept of image is central to the selection of many nonfood expense items. Why is this true? What types of operations do you think must be most concerned with this issue? Which do you think might be the least concerned? Why?

2. You have just been given the opportunity to build a new hotel. Discuss the specifications you will need for (1) housekeeping products, (2) the type of fabrics you will use for bedspreads, and (3) the types of amenities you will have in each room. Justify your product selections.

3. The two dishwashers in your kitchen have finally stopped working. Assume you have no equipment program. What do you do with the dishwashers? Do you find someone to repair them or buy new ones? What are the advantages/disadvantages of buying used versus new? What other factors will help you make your decision?

Chapter 26
Services
After reading this chapter, you should be able to:
- Identify management considerations surrounding the selection and procurement of services.
- List the types of services that might be purchased by a hospitality operator.
- Outline the general procedures used when purchasing services.
- Describe the major selection factors for services.

Outline
1. Introduction
   - In most hospitality operations, unit managers purchase the services
2. Management Considerations
   - Not all costs are fixed costs; managers do have some discretion
     - Managers should spend as much time purchasing services as they do with other purchasing activities
   - Evaluating a service provider's performance can be difficult
   - Decide whether to buy a service or provide it themselves
     - Conduct a cost-benefit analysis
     - Hospitality operators purchase a service when one (or more) of the following apply
       - The service is impossible for them to do
       - It is inconvenient to provide it themselves
     - "Outsourcing"
     - If leasing the facility, the landlord may provide some of the services
       - CAM fee
   - Examining a service provider's background and abilities
     - Licenses
     - Contact Better Business Bureau
   - Consider the advantages and disadvantages of using moonlighters
     - Part-time persons who work odd evening hours while holding down another job
     - Cannot always provide the services when needed
   - Other concerns include
     - Managers may have to permit strangers on the premises
     - May have to give strangers access to confidential information
     - Allowing a third party to have direct control over some aspect of the business
3. General Procedures in Service Purchasing
   - Decide which services to purchase; prepare a specification for each
   - Bid buy services
     - Carries inherent dangers
     - The most important aspect is to get what operation needs
4. Typical Services That Hospitality Operators Purchase
   - Waste removal
     - Primary purpose of waste disposal is to maintain a neat and sanitary garbage area
     - Pickup schedule
     - If operators have a grease trap, they will find it convenient to use a waste removal firm to provide this service
     - Some waste removal companies may pay companies for their waste
   - Financial
     - Usually have flexibility for loan capital, checking services, or other financial services

- Need bankers who will provide checking accounts, petty cash accounts, payroll accounts, loans, cash management techniques, computer services and monitor benefit packages for employees
- "Grow up" with a local banker
- Groundskeeping
  - Few operators are able to provide their own landscaping, snow removal, or parking lot maintenance
  - When operators purchase landscaping service, they must be specific about what they want done and when they want it done
  - Landscaping services often have a firm rate schedule
- Pest control
  - One of the trickiest control areas in the entire hospitality industry
  - Best strategy is to contract for a weekly or monthly visit
  - Purchasing this service is preferable to performing it themselves
  - The cost of pest control service is small compared with the problems
- Advertising
  - Most operations use some sort of advertising
  - Keep in mind intended audience
  - Price is directly related to the size of the audience
  - Must consider cost per potential customer reached by or influenced by the ad
  - Option for operators to trade products or services for advertising
  - The use of soft-drink company signs and printing
  - Sponsorships
  - Advertising agency or media-buying service
  - Many experienced hospitality operators prefer using an intermediary when purchasing advertising services
  - Newspaper ads
  - Radio ads
  - Television ads
  - Web ads
  - Magazine ads
  - Telephone directories
    - The price of most directory advertising is fixed
    - Most common directory is the yellow pages
    - Operators should consider the cost, the number of years it has been published, the target audience, and the way it is distributed to readers
    - When receiving invoices that look like they are from a directory listing, be very cautious about paying for any service that may have not been ordered
  - Printed Brochures, Matchbooks, and Menus
    - Brochures and flyers are quite useful in some circumstances
    - Publication rates are usually fairly standard
    - Operators may wish to hire graphic artists to design a logo or pictorial layout, and an editor to develop the wording style
    - Most operators purchase matchbooks, swizzle sticks and napkins emblazoned with their logo
  - Outdoor ads
    - Billboards
  - Direct mail advertising
- Consulting
  - Consultants abound in the hospitality industry

- o Used whenever the task to be performed is complicated, highly technical, not part of the owner-manager's daily routine
- o Large organizations often hire in-house consultants as permanent staff
- o Operators can use some type of bid buying when purchasing these services
- o Be clear about what is needed
- o Before purchasing a consulting service, operators might try to get it free
- Decorating and remodeling
- Maintenance
  - o Endless variety of repair and maintenance services
  - o Typical hospitality operators tend to purchase one or more maintenance contracts
  - o Be certain that the service is available as advertised
- Vending machine
  - o Some operations use coin-operated or smart-card operated vending machines
  - o In many cases, the machines come with established agreements
  - o Some of the concerns about vending machines include
    - ▪ Whether or not to have such machines on their property
    - ▪ Potential quality differences among competing companies' machines and the products
    - ▪ Commission split
    - ▪ Option: Buy machines and do all the work
  - o A large operation can contract with an intermediary who will oversee the vending-machine program for all the company's individual locations across the United States
- Insurance
  - o No single, all-inclusive insurance policy exists
  - o Must purchase more than one
  - o Operators can purchase additional insurance policies at their discretion
    - ▪ Health or life insurance for company personnel
    - ▪ Employee benefits
    - ▪ Extra insurance on expensive antiques, works of art, and furnishings
  - o When evaluating insurance coverage, consider three major factors
    - ▪ The extent of the coverage, or amount of deductible
    - ▪ Reimbursable losses
    - ▪ Conditions to be satisfied before collecting money
  - o Before contracting with an insurance company
    - ▪ Determine the skill of the person handling the claims
    - ▪ Number of policies operators can obtain from one source
  - o Buy insurance directly
  - o Exclusive insurance agent
  - o Consider joining a risk-purchasing group
  - o Consult legal counsel before making a decision
- Laundry and linen supply
  - o If operators use linens and uniforms
    - ▪ Buy their own and purchase a laundry service
    - ▪ Purchase the laundry service and rent the fabrics
    - ▪ Purchase their own fabrics and laundry machines and do the work
  - o If decision is to rent linen and laundry service, evaluate supplier
    - ▪ Length of contract
    - ▪ Service schedule
    - ▪ How seasonal fluctuations are handled
    - ▪ Variety and quality of products offered

- Overall cost of the service
- Cost of lost, damaged, or stolen products
- Cleaning
  - Several specified contract cleaning services are available
    - Exhaust hood
    - Degreasing
    - Window
    - Carpet and upholstery
    - Concrete cleaning
  - Cleaning is one service that hospitality operations can perform
    - Every day cleaning
    - Weekly or monthly cleaning tasks that require specialized equipment should become the responsibility of a contract cleaner
  - Advantage of contract cleaners
    - Eliminates the need to purchase and store heavy equipment and supplies
    - Eliminates expensive labor
    - Relatively easy to evaluate
  - Disadvantage of contract cleaners
    - Lack of complete control over employees
    - Cost
    - Laxity of hospitality operators to inspect their work
    - Using amateurs to do the work
    - Some cleaners have difficulty maintaining staff of their own
5. Another Word About Security When Buying Services
   - Shady characters are always ready to sell hospitality operators a nonexistent product
   - Hospitality operators do not usually buy questionable advertised bargains
   - Operators should check bills for services and initial them before giving them to the bookkeeper
   - Extra invoices
   - Deposits before work is performed and then service provider never returns
   - Small businesses, rather than large firms, are usually targets for dishonest persons

True/False

T F 1. Bid buying can be monetarily rewarding when purchasing services.

T F 2. Hospitality operations typically purchase human resources services.

T F 3. The primary purpose of waste disposal is to maintain an unsanitary garbage area.

T F 4. The primary disadvantage to outdoor advertising is the community's concern about "visual pollution."

T F 5. Accounting and bookkeeping are traditionally two services that hospitality operators buy.

T F 6. Banner ads are ads that are placed on other related companies' websites.

T F 7. Purchasing services always involves fixed costs.

T F 8. A challenge to purchasing outside services is evaluating the service performance.

T F 9. Outsourcing involves identifying work that is central to a hospitality operation's core competency.

T F 10. Guidelines for purchasing services may vary depending on the service.

Fill-in-the-Blank

1. Four services that hospitality operators typically purchase are _____, _____, _____, and _____.

2. Tenants with businesses in a shopping area usually pay rent in addition to a _____ fee.

3. When purchasing insurance, an arrangement that enables individuals to become part of a larger group to reduce insurance costs for all of the group members, is known as a _____ arrangement.

4. Part-time employees who work odd hours while holding down another full-time job are knows as _____.

5. Three specialized contract cleaning services that an operator might use are _____, _____, and _____.

6. To save money when buying insurance, an operator may purchase _____ from the insurance company.

7. The most common telephone directory is the _____.

8. _____ advertising is often too expensive for hospitality operators.

9. Groundskeeping services usually include _____, _____, and _____ services.

10. To see if any complaints are lodged against a service provider, the operator may contact the local _____ for that information.

Multiple Choice

1. Disadvantages to hiring cleaning services include all of the following except:
    a. management's lack of control over workers
    b. the service may be quite inexpensive
    c. hospitality operators tend not to inspect the work done in their properties
    d. contract cleaners may be amateurs

2. Hospitality operators usually purchase a consultant's services when:
    a. the task to be performed is very complicated and highly technical
    b. the task not part of the company's normal routine
    c. other operators are doing it
    d. both "a" and "b"

3. The following is a major concern for management when purchasing services:
   a. managers must realize that services are fixed costs
   b. evaluating a service provider's performance is not difficult
   c. making the decision to provide their own service or buy it
   d. need to examine the service providers background

4. CAM stands for:
   a. common area maintenance
   b. common application maintenance
   c. customary area maintenance
   d. common area management

5. A contract that stipulates that the service provider can attach a lien to the entire property if clients fail to pay for the work performed is known as a:
   a. "take back" contract
   b. lien-sale contract
   c. a co-op agreement
   d. none of the above

6. Moonlighters tend to dominate which service field?
   a. cleaning
   b. groundskeeping
   c. decorating and remodeling
   d. financial

7. Some major concerns for managers with vending machines include:
   a. the decision to buy and maintain or lease vending machines
   b. quality differences among competing vending companies
   c. the decision to offer vending services on their property
   d. all of the above

8. When evaluating insurance services, what should operators consider?
   a. the extent of the coverage
   b. how many people will handle the policy
   c. where the insurance company is located
   d. if the insurance company is part of an insurance network

9. Large operations, when considering laundry service, typically choose which option?
   a. purchase laundry service and rent fabrics/uniforms/linens
   b. purchase their own fabric and laundry machines and do their own work
   c. buy their own fabric and purchase a laundry service
   d. none of the above

10. Laundry service suppliers should be evaluated based on all of the following factors except:
    a. length of contract
    b. variety and quality of products offered
    c. type of disposable napkins they carry
    d. the overall cost of the service

Apply Your Knowledge

1. You have just purchased an entirely new air conditioning system for your property. The supplier of the air conditioning product has offered you both a service agreement and a maintenance agreement. Which option would you choose and why? Discuss the advantages and disadvantages of each agreement.

2. Most hospitality operations engage in some form of advertising for their business, and it is a service that many operations purchase. As the owner of a new restaurant in town, you need to advertise so that people will know you are open. Discuss two types of advertising that you would utilize. Why did you choose those two? Provide examples of how you would use the advertising that you have chosen and why you think it will be effective.

3. You are preparing your hotel for its grand opening, and are contemplating which services you are going to purchase. You have decided on financial services, cleaning services, pest control, and laundry and linen supply. Which of your services will be appropriate for bid buying? Why? Which of your services are not appropriate for bid buying? Why not?

Chapter 27
Furniture, Fixtures and Equipment

After reading this chapter, you should be able to:

- Identify management considerations surrounding the selection and procurement of furniture, fixtures, and equipment.
- Outline the general procedures used when purchasing furniture, fixtures, and equipment.
- Describe the major selection factors for furniture, fixtures, and equipment.

Outline

1. Introduction
   - Furniture, fixtures, and equipment (FFE) are sometimes referred to as "capital items" or long-life items
   - Selection and procurement procedures involve principles enumerated in this text
   - Operators are conscious of even the smallest potential for error
2. Management Considerations
   - Determining FFE needs appears to be a relatively easy task for managers
   - FFE major concerns
     - Future plans
     - Growth aspirations
     - Capitalizing an operating expense
     - Selecting the person who should select the FFE
     - Reconditioning versus replacing the items
     - Impulse purchases
3. General Procedures in FFE Purchasing
   - Often, operators do not prepare formal specifications for replacement
     - Attend trade shows, competitors' operations, catalogs, trade papers
     - Operators have past experience to guide them
     - Operators examine replacement FFE closely before making purchase decisions
   - When a major FFE purchase is contemplated, specifications are normally necessary
   - The FFE specification
     - Supplier services
     - Instructions to bidders
     - General conditions
     - Specific conditions
     - Detailed drawings
   - Once specifications are prepared, make a list of potential suppliers and develop an approved-supplier list
4. Selection Factors
   - Intended use
   - Exact name
     - Details the specific type of FFE they need
     - Model numbers
   - Lifetime cost
     - FFE purchase decision is a long-term investment
     - Besides the AP Price, it is imperative that operators consider
       - Trade-in value of old FFE
       - Delivery costs
       - Installation and testing costs
       - Relevant operating costs
       - Potential operating savings

- The trade-in value of the new FFE
  - "Personal equipment rental firm"
  - Operators should be skeptical of unusually low AP price quotations
  - Lowball bids can take many forms
- Potential operating savings
  - Quite often, operators purchase a piece of equipment primarily to effect a savings in operating expenses
  - Management can control several operating expenses that are good candidates for possible future reductions
    - Cost of merchandise
    - Cost of labor
    - Cost of energy
    - Cost of taxes
    - Cost of waste removal
  - "Net present value" procedure
    - Takes into account the time value of money
    - Predicting future operating savings is very difficult
- Direct purchase
  - Go straight to the manufacturer and purchase FFE items
    - AP price may be lower
    - Chances are buyer will need to provide maintenance crew
  - Manufacturers may not sell directly to the end user
    - Don't want to maintain credit or provide local support
- Demonstration models
  - Manufacturers and dealers use FFE models for demonstration purposes
  - Operators might be able to purchase these items and save a considerable amount of money
  - If they buy this type of FFE, they must
    - Put up the AP price in cash
    - Take the item as-is
    - Provide transportation and/or installation
  - Operators must also consider the downside
- Equipment programs
  - Operators can use a company's machinery as long as they are using the food, beverage, or cleaning product that the machinery dispenses
  - Tying agreement
  - A supplier may or may not charge a surcharge for using the equipment
  - In most instances, equipment programs have been advantageous to hospitality operators
- Custom FFE
  - Very expensive
  - May not be worth the extra cost and inconvenience
  - Save some expense by finding a dealer that has merchandise that is part standard and part customized
  - Potential advantages of customized FFE
    - Operating savings
    - Easier to operate, maintain and clean
    - More attractive
    - Custom image
    - Obtain exactly what is needed
    - Lifetime costs can be more attractive

- New versus used FFE
    - May come across merchandise that could have suffered little or no use
    - In most cases, operators can purchase items for a fraction of original selling prices
    - At times, operators hire an auctioneer to liquidate FFE
    - Some operators seek out auctioneers
    - The potential advantage of used merchandise is the reduction in purchase price
    - Disadvantages of used merchandise
        - Obsolete merchandise
        - An energy guzzler
        - An item that inefficiently uses floor space
        - Merchandise that is expensive to maintain
        - Item that does not meet current fire, health and safety, and building codes
    - Operators must also consider
        - Time required to seek out the bargain
        - Time needed to examine items before purchasing
        - Item lacks guarantee
        - Possibility that replacement parts are no longer available
        - Possibility of damage to company's image
        - Inability to predict the amount of money needed to recondition the product
- Versatility
    - Equipment that can do more than one job
    - Cost of space is expensive
- Compactness
    - Operators cannot ignore convenience and space-saving capabilities
- Compatibility
    - Hospitality operators should attempt to ensure that new purchases will intermingle easily with their current stock
- Appearance
    - Image is a precious commodity
    - Must do whatever is feasible to protect and enhance
- Brand name
    - Most operators use this selection factor almost exclusively to purchase replacement FFE
    - Brand names can have a positive effect on the operators' image
    - "Halo effect"
- Portability
    - Very important selection factor for kitchen equipment
    - Ability to move the items for maintenance
    - Replace a broken item with loaner item
    - Portable equipment tends to retain its value over the long run
    - Cost more because of convenience
- Ease of cleaning
    - All FFE items must be cleaned periodically
    - Clean FFE should last longer under normal operating conditions
    - Equipment that is not properly designed could harbor bacteria, pests, and dirt; transfer unwanted flavors and aromas to other products
    - Self-cleaning devices
- Ease of maintenance
    - Most equipment requires some sort of repair and maintenance
    - Directly reflects the total operating costs over the life of the items

- Degree of automation
  - Labor-saving opportunity
  - Operators should judge automated equipment in its ability to provide standardized products
- Availability of replacement parts
  - Hospitality operators must ensure that an inventory of spare parts is available for the FFE they purchase
  - Time lag between ordering and delivery of parts
  - Should assume replacement parts are not available if FFE is used
  - Might experience difficulty in finding parts and service for technologically unique equipment or customized FFE
- Supplier services
  - "Service after the sale"
  - FFE items will need repair, maintenance service, and replacement parts during the warranty period
  - Service appears to be the most important of the selection factors
    - Must have a trustworthy supplier
  - After the warranty period and break-in period expire, operators may wish to engage other service providers for maintenance
  - When operators purchase FFE directly, they may have to forgo any service after the sale
- Employee attitude and skill level
  - Before purchasing complicated equipment, operators must ensure that the staff is able to comprehend the operating procedures
  - Must also be certain that everyone will accept the new equipment
- Energy source
  - Hospitality operators can run machinery using various energy sources
    - Natural gas
    - Electricity
    - Steam oil
    - Solar power
- Excess capacity
  - Consider the potential growth of their business when purchasing FFE
  - If larger equipment is available today at an attractive AP price, operators might consider purchasing it
    - If not, they probably should avoid these items for several reasons
      - Can often buy equipment with add-on capability
      - They will waste money with a larger-than-necessary piece of equipment
      - They will have capital tied up in the larger equipment
      - They have no guarantee that their business will increase
  - Adding on to the physical space when customer count increases is more difficult
- Add-on capabilities
  - If an increase in business is anticipated, might consider purchasing items that can be modified and adapted to service additional business
  - Discuss needs with supplier and agree to purchase the added capacity later on
- Warranty
  - Unusual for suppliers to sell any FFE without a manufacturer's warranty
  - Typical warranty covers parts and repair for 12 to 24 months from date of shipment
  - Main issue with warranty is convenience, or lack thereof
  - Warranties are only as good as the manufacturer's or dealer's intention to honor them

- Code compliance
    - Local governments normally enforce several laws governing fire, health and safety, and building procedures
    - FFE must meet existing legal codes
    - Buyers normally look for seals of approval when purchasing FFE
        - UL
        - AGA
        - NFPA
        - ASME
5. Financing the FFE Purchase
    - Operators must devote as much thought to the financing of the purchase as they do the various selection factors
    - Purchasing FFE is not an everyday occurrence
    - Operators need to be able to finance FFE purchases
        - Normal cash flow of the operation
        - Credit arrangements
            - Installment payment plans
            - One-third of purchase price as a down payment
            - Make monthly payments
        - Credit cards
            - Interest rates are much higher
        - FFE as collateral
            - Expensive alternative
            - Require a large down payment
        - Lease agreements
            - More expensive than buying
            - Rent-to-own plans
            - Does have advantages
                - Don't have to put up large amounts of money as down payment
                - Can experiment with new technology without making a long-term purchase commitment

True/False

T F 1. ASME stands for American Society of Managerial Engineers

T F 2. A capital item is a short-life item.

T F 3. Capital items include furniture, fixtures, and equipment.

T F 4. FFE buyers tend to use product specifications as opposed to purchase specifications.

T F 5. The net present value procedure takes into account the time value of money.

T F 6. A company producing a customized item for a hospitality operation may go out of business. This is a major advantage of ordering customized products.

T F 7. A major disadvantage of purchasing used FFE is the potential savings in cost.

T F 8. Portability and ease of cleaning are two factors to consider when purchasing FFE.

T F 9. The typical warranty covers parts and repair for 12 to 24 months from date of shipment.

T F 10. Leasing televisions and laundry equipment, instead of buying them, is a common practice in the foodservice industry.

Fill-in-the-Blank
1. CAD stands for _____. It is used to help design equipment layouts.

2. A dealer who is prepared to provide, free of charge, all the advice and assistance operators need, as long as they purchase all of their FFE from that dealer, is called a _____ dealer.

3. _____ is the length of time during which operators cannot profitably conduct business because they are still waiting for some FFE to be delivered and installed.

4. Furniture, fixtures, and equipment are sometimes referred to as _____ items.

5. FFE products that are expected to last at least one year and, perhaps as long as 20 years, are called _____ items.

6. An agreement which grants the dealer the right to foreclose and take back the FFE item if the operators fail to make their installment payments, is called a _____ agreement.

7. _____ provides sanitation certification and a seal of approval for sanitation equipment.

8. If operators have a positive experience with a specific brand or supplier, they will mostly likely buy the same brand in the future. This is known as the _____ effect.

9. Manufacturers and dealers sometimes sell _____ items, which are items they are willing to sell for a fraction of the original AP prices.

10. NFPA stands for _____.

Multiple Choice
1. Which of the following is a disadvantage associated with purchasing used FFE?
    a. the equipment might save energy
    b. used items are quick and easy to find
    c. the merchandise may be out of date
    d. replacement parts will be readily available

2. Customized FFE may be very expensive. Costs associated with customized FFE include which of the following?
    a. no future trade-in value will exist
    b. fabricator may go out of business making servicing the item difficult
    c. the item may have several bugs and be difficult to repair
    d. all of the above

3. Selection factors for FFE include which of the following?
    a. employee skill and ability
    b. demonstration models
    c. compactness
    d. all of the above

4. "Should operators buy kitchen equipment that handles the current customer load only, or should they purchase excess capacity equipment now?" In other words, should the buyer purchase:
   a. excess capacity
   b. more equipment
   c. larger equipment
   d. more expensive equipment

5. FFE may be purchased several ways. One such procedure is using contract supply houses. These are known as:
   a. contract supply arrangements
   b. co-op arrangements
   c. design consultants
   d. one-stop shopping

6. Which of the following are concerns that managers may have before deciding to purchase major FFE?
   a. will the operator actually need the same FFE in the future?
   b. will the large expense today reduce costs in the future?
   c. deciding who in the operation should purchase the FFE
   d. all of the above

7. Trade shows are a popular place to evaluate new FFE items. Managers should evaluate what major factors when looking at items in a trade show?
   a. functionality
   b. total cost
   c. the color
   d. all of the above

8. Hotel/casinos, as well as foodservice operations, use this software to design the layout of their operations:
   a. CDD
   b. CAD
   c. DAC
   d. CAAD

9. Which of the following costs are not important when considering the purchase of FFE?
   a. delivery costs
   b. relevant operations costs
   c. manufacturers suggested retail price
   d. installation costs

10. The net present value procedure:
    a. takes into account the time value of money
    b. estimates future interest rates
    c. is the as-purchased price
    d. all of the above

Apply Your Knowledge

1.   The restaurant that you have just purchased needs complete remodeling and the kitchen equipment is old. Before purchasing any FFE, as the manger, discuss with your employees whether you should purchase new FFE, reconditioned FFE, or used FFE. Explain to them the advantages and disadvantages of all three types. What is your final decision based on those advantages/disadvantages?

2.   If an operator purchases a natural gas–powered stove, it will usually be more expensive than a similar electrically powered one. The operator decides, however, that the extra expense is worth it. What would the operator decide to spend more money in this case?

3.   When opening your new foodservice establishment, and purchasing all of the tables for the operation, discuss why portability might be an important consideration.

Answer Key
Chapter 1
True/False

1. F	2. F	3. T	4. T	5. F
6. F	7. T	8. T	9. T	10. T

Fill-in-the-Blank

1. selection; procurement; selection; procurement
2.

Hospitality Operation	**Commercial/Non-Commercial**	**Example**
profit-oriented	commercial	caterer
institutional	non-commercial	Girl Scout camp
military	non-commercial	military base

3. business to business; B2B; business to consumer; B2C; e-procurement
4. co-op buying
5. aggregate purchasing company; group purchasing organization
6. central distribution center; commissary

Multiple Choice

1. d	2. c	3. d	4. c	5. a

Chapter 2
True/False

1. F	2. T	3. T	4. T	5. T
6. F	7. T	8. T	9. T	10. F

Fill-in-the-Blank

1. middleman; intermediary; customer relations management; CRM
2. Uniform Resource Locator; URL
3. World Wide Web; U.S. Department of Agriculture
4. point-of-sale
5. prime vendor
6. disintermediation
7. radio frequency identification tags; RFIDS
8. product identification
9. Efficient Foodservice Response (EFR)
10. marketing boards

Multiple Choice

1. a	2. a	3. a	4. d	5. d
6. c	7. b	8. c	9. a	10. b

Chapter 3
True/False

1. F	2. T	3. T	4. T	5. F
6. F	7. T	8. T	9. T	10. T

Fill-in-the-Blank

1. alcoholic beverage commission
2. broadline
3. storefront dealer
4. Efficient Foodservice Response (EFR); Efficient Consumer Response (ECR); Quick Response (QR)
5. exclusive territories
6. tied-house laws
7. full-line; full-service dealer
8. commissary

9. end-user services
10. direct buying

Multiple Choice

1. c	2. a	3. b	4. d	5. c
6. d	7. a	8. b	9. d	10. d

Chapter 4
True/False

1. T	2. F	3. T	4. T	5. T
6. F	7. F	8. T	9. F	10. T

Fill-in-the-Blank

1. Sherman Antitrust Act; Federal Trade Commission; Clayton Act
2. Wholesome Meat Act; Wholesome Poultry Products Act
3. express; implied
4. Perishable Agricultural Commodities Act
5. tying agreements; exclusive dealing
6. Food and Drug Administration
7. Hart Act
8. Marine Mammal Protection Act
9. controlled atmosphere packaging; modified atmosphere packaging
10. offering discounts to certain buyers and not others; setting qualification levels for quality discounts so high they can only be met by a few buyers; practicing predatory pricing or pricing goods or services so low that other suppliers are put out of business

Multiple Choice

1. d	2. b	3. c	4. c	5. c
6. b	7. b	8. c	9. d	10. c

Chapter 5
True/False

1. F	2. T	3. T	4. F	5. T
6. F	7. T	8. T	9. T	10. T

Fill-in-the-Blank

1. backdoor selling
2. supplier selection; sourcing
3. value analysis
4. make-or-buy analysis; high cost
5. one-stop shopping; trade relations
6. forecasting; what-if analysis
7. Certified Foodservice Professional (CFSP)
8. back order
9. optimize; minimizing
10. small stop

Multiple Choice

1. c	2. c	3. d	4. c	5. d
6. b	7. a	8. c	9. c	10. d

Chapter 6
True/False

1. T	2. F	3. T	4. T	5. T
6. T	7. F	8. F	9. T	10. F

Fill-in-the-Blank
1. controlling
2. direct control; indirect control
3. co-op purchasing; shared buying
4. user-buyer; medium-sized independent
5. vice president of purchasing; approved suppliers

Multiple Choice

1. c	2. a	3. b	4. c	5. d

Chapter 7
True/False

1. F	2. T	3. F	4. T	5. T
6. F	7. T	8. F	9. T	10. T

Fill-in-the-Blank
1. back order; stockout
2. backdoor selling
3. conceptual skills; interpersonal or human skills; technical skills
4. reciprocity
5. inventory turnover; beginning; ending
6. objectives of the purchasing function
7. job description; job specification
8. steward sales
9. hospitals, employee feeding programs, prisons
10. technical

Multiple Choice

1. d	2. c	3. a	4. b	5. c
6. c	7. b	8. d	9. c	10. b

Chapter 8
True/False

1. T	2. F	3. F	4. T	5. T
6. T	7. T	8. F	9. F	10. T

Fill-in-the-Blank
1. sell-by; freshness; pull; best-if-used-by
2. "or equivalent"; equal to or better
3. low balling
4. brand awareness, packer's brand, packer's grade
5. wide tolerance between grades; grader discretion; deceiving appearance of products; possible irrelevance of grades to EP cost; graders might not take into account such items as delivery schedules or packaging; raw food items may not have consistent grades throughout the year; lack of uniformity among terms; lack of a specific regional designation
6. slab-packed
7. weight range; trim; form; yield
8. USDA Acceptance Service
9. supplier services may be included in the specification and add to the AP price but may not add overall value; inadvertent discrimination may be written into the specification; the specification

may request a quality difficult to obtain; may rely too much on government standards; food specs change

10.   performance requirements or intended use

Multiple Choice

1. c	2. b	3. a	4. c	5. d
6. c	7. a	8. a	9. d	10. c

Chapter 9

True/False

1. T	2. F	3. F	4. T	5. F
6. T	7. F	8. T	9. T	10. T

Fill-in-the-Blank

1.   lead time; just-in-time
2.   PF = 16 oz. / amount of ingredient need for one serving in ounces
3.   PD = PF x ingredient's edible yield percentage
4.   reorder point; ROP
5.   capital cost; opportunity cost
6.   economic order point; EOP
7.   number of customers; PD for that ingredient
8.   forecasting
9.   inventory turnover
10. stockout costs

Multiple Choice

1. d	2. a	3. d	4. c	5. b
6. a	7. d	8. a	9. a	10. c

Chapter 10

True/False

1. F	2. T	3. T	4. F	5. T
6. F	7. T	8. T	9. F	10. T

Fill-in-the-Blank

1.   blanket order
2.   cost-plus purchasing; landed cost
3.   daisy chain
4.   bottom-line, firm-price purchasing
5.   cash rebate
6.   hedging
7.   exchange bartering
8.   make-or-buy analysis
9.   product substitution
10.   "as-is, where-is"

Multiple Choice

1. a	2. d	3. b	4. c	5. d
6. b	7. a	8. b	9 c	10. d

Chapter 11

True/False

1. T	2. F	3. F	4. T	5. T

Fill-in-the-Blank

1.   concerned

2. credit risk; cash-on-delivery; COD
3. escrow
4. good cash management
5. credit period

Multiple Choice

1. a	2. c	3. d	4. a	5. b

Chapter 12
True/False

1. F	2. T	3. F	4. T	5. T
6. F	7. T	8. F	9. F	10. T

Fill-in-the-Blank
1. product
2. judgment
3. daily
4. fixed bid
5. forward buying
6. e-marketplaces
7. morning
8. credit terms
9. satisfied
10. common sense; company policy

Multiple Choice

1. d	2. d	3. a	4. c	5. b
6. d	7. c	8. d	9. d	10. b

Chapter 13
True/False

1. T	2. F	3. T	4. F	5. T
6. F	7. F	8. T	9. F	10. F

Fill-in-the-Blank
1. purchase order or requisition
2. par stock approach
3. limited purchase order; (LPO)
4. expediting
5. blanket ordering
6. purchase requisition
7. stock requisition
8. buying
9. buyer
10. management

Multiple Choice

1. d	2. c	3. a	4. c	5. d
6. a	7. b	8. d	9. c	10. a

Chapter 14
True/False

1. F	2. F	3. F	4. T	5. T
6. F	7. T	8. F	9. T	10. F

Fill-in-the-Blank
1. backhauling
2. receiving sheet
3. standing-order receiving; becoming too relaxed
4. pick-up memo
5. slacked out
6. equal to facing layer
7. stock rotation
8. meat tags; stock requisitions
9. shrink allowance
10. expiration date

Multiple Choice

1. d	2. a	3. c	4. b	5. a
6. b	7. c	8. a	9. d	10. b

Chapter 15
True/False

1. F	2. T	3. T	4. F	5. T
6. T	7. F	8. F	9. T	10. T

Fill-in-the-Blank
1. National Restaurant Association
2. stock requisition
3. critical item inventory analysis; auditing the inventory; sales product analysis
4. direct purchases; directs
5. temperature; humidity
6. ingredient room; working storeroom
7. issuing procedure
8. beginning inventory + purchases – ending inventory – other credits
9. computerized management information system (MIS)
10. classify; organize

Multiple Choice

1. d	2. d	3. a	4. b	5. d

Chapter 16
True/False

1. F	2. F	3. T	4. F	5. T
6. F	7. F	8. F	9. F	10. F

Fill-in-the-Blank
1. padding
2. kickback
3. authorized persons
4. cash
5. shopper or spotter
6. bonding company
7. invoice scam
8. inventory substitution
9. e-mails
10. prosecute

Multiple Choice

1. a	2. c	3. a	4. c	5. d
6. a	7. b	8. d	9. c	10. a

Chapter 17
True/False

1. T	2. F	3. T	4. F	5. T
6. T	7. F	8. T	9. F	10. F

Fill-in-the-Blank
1.   meat
2.   hundred
3.   variety
4.   No. 1
5.   packers' brands
6.   sizes
7.   5
8.   layered
9.   wax
10. organic

Multiple Choice

1. d	2. a	3. b	4. b	5. a
6. d	7. b	8. b	9. a	10. c

Chapter 18
True/False

1. F	2. F	3. F	4. F	5. T
6. F	7. T	8. T	9. F	10. F

Fill-in-the-Blank
1.   predictable; fluctuate
2.   labor; energy; overhead
3.   mold; broken pieces; odd appearance
4. 10° F
5.   pesticides; synthetic; sewage sludge; bioengineering; irradiation
6.   dry; 50° F; 70°F
7.   heat
8.   suppliers; shelf life
9.   drained weight; servable weight
10. labor savings; food safety; storage

Multiple Choice

1. c	2. d	3. d	4. a	5. d
6. b	7. a	8. d	9. a	10. b

Chapter 19
True/False

1. F	2. F	3. T	4. F	5. F
6. F	7. F	8. F	9. T	10. F

Fill-in-the-Blank
1.   evaporated milk; sweetened condensed milk
2.   shelf-stable; ultra-high temperatures; UHT; ultra-pasteurized; UP
3.   bovine somatotropin; bST; Recombinant Bovine Growth Hormone; rBGH
4.   overrun

5.   fortified milk
6.   "French"
7.   perishable
8.   milk solids content
9.   certified
10. free-market area; noncontrolled state; controlled state

Multiple Choice

1. a	2. d	3. d	4. c	5. c
6. c	7. b	8. b	9. c	10. a

Chapter 20
True/False

1. F	2. T	3. T	4. F	5. T
6. F	7. T	8. T	9. F	10. T

Fill-in-the-Blank
1.   candling
2.   albumen
3.   egg products
4.   Cryovac; Cryovac bags
5.   size; uniformity

Multiple Choice

1. c	2. d	3. b	4. a	5. b

Chapter 21
True False

1. F	2. F	3. T	4. T	5. F
6. T	7. F	8. T	9. T	10. F

Fill-in-the-Blank
1.   irradiation
2.   ice pack method
3.   Food Safety & Inspection Service (FSIS)
4.   B
5.   Perdue; Tyson; Foster Farms
6.   ice pack procedure
7.   USDA's acceptance service
8.   conversion weight
9.   commodity
10. natural

Multiple Choice

1. d	2. c	3. b	4. c	5. a
6. d	7. a	8. b	9. a	10. b

Chapter 22
True/False

1. T	2. T	3. F	4. T	5. F
6. F	7. F	8. T	9. F	10. F

Fill-in-the-Blank
1.   Seafood Handbook; Seafood Business; Seafood price-current
2.   closed shells
3.   aquaculture
4.   32°F; 64

5.   National Marine Fisheries Service
6.   C
7.   cans; bottles; moisture/vapor proof material
8.   slacked-out
9.   substitution; convenience
10.   14-16 pieces

Multiple Choice

1. a	2. d	3. d	4. c	5. c
6. a	7. b	8. d	9. a	10. b

Chapter 23
True/False

1. T	2. T	3. F	4. T	5. F
6. T	7. F	8. T	9. F	10. F

Fill-in-the-Blank

1.   sausage; variety meats
2.   Federal Meat Inspection Act
3.   edible portion cost
5.   4
6.   Institutional Meat Purchase Specifications
7.   Meat Buyers Guide
8.   prime; choice; good; utility
9.   curing; smoking; nitrites (two of the three)
10.   comminuting

Multiple Choice

1. a	2. d	3. c	4. a	5. b
6. d	7. d	8. c	9. c	10. d

Chapter 24
True/False

1. F	2. T	3. F	4. F	5. T
6. F	7. T	8. F	9. T	10. T

Fill-in-the-Blank

1.   proof
2.   liquor
3.   call
4.   juice
5.   premix
6.   nitrogen-flushing
7.   50
8.   driving while intoxicated
9.   license
10.   Dram Shop

Multiple Choice

1. d	2. b	3. c	4. a	5. d
6. b	7. b	8. a	9. c	10. d

Chapter 25
True/False

1. F	2. T	3. F	4. T	5. T
6. T	7. F	8. T	9. F	10. T

Fill-in-the-Blank
1. bid
2. Occupational Safety and Health Administration (OSHA)
3. par stock; appropriate suppliers
4. stockless purchase
5. cleaning supplies; cleaning tools; maintenance supplies; permanent ware; single-service disposable ware; preparation and service utensils; fabrics; other paper products; miscellaneous
6. cleaning
7. capitalized
8. minimum order
9. length of service
10. equipment program

Multiple Choice

1. d	2. d	3. a	4. c	5. a
6. d	7. b	8. d	9. c	10. c

Chapter 26
True/False

1. T	2. F	3. F	4. T	5. T
6. T	7. F	8. T	9. F	10. T

Fill-in-the-Blank
1. waste removal; financial; groundskeeping; pest control; advertising; consulting; decorating/remodeling; maintenance; vending machine; insurance; laundry and linen supply; cleaning
2. common area maintenace
3. co-op purchasing
4. moonlighting
5. exhaust hood; degreasing; window; carpet and upholstery; concrete
6. directly
7. yellow pages
8. television
9. landscaping; snow removal; parking lot maintenance
10. Better Business Bureau

Multiple Choice

1. b	2. d	3. c	4. a	5. b
6. c	7. d	8. a	9. b	10. c

Chapter 27
True/False

1. F	2. F	3. T	4. F	5. T
6. F	7. F	8. T	9. T	10. F

Fill-in-the-Blank
1. computer aided design
2. design/build
3. downtime
4. capital items
5. capital or long-life
6. security
7. NSF International
8. halo
9. freight damaged
10. National Fire Protection Association

Multiple Choice

1. c	2. d	3. d	4. a	5. b
6. d	7. d	8. b	9. c	10. a